T5-BAF-949

PUBLISHED FOR THE MALONE SOCIETY BY
OXFORD UNIVERSITY PRESS

GREAT CLARENDON STREET, OXFORD OX2 6DP

Oxford New York
Athens Auckland Bangkok Bogotá Bombay Buenos Aires
Cape Town Chennai Dar es Salaam Delhi Florence Hong Kong Istanbul
Karachi Kolkata Kuala Lumpur Madrid Melbourne Mexico City Mumbai
Nairobi Paris São Paulo Shanghai Singapore Taipei Tokyo Toronto Warsaw
with associated companies in
Berlin Ibadan

British Library Cataloguing in Publication Data
A catalogue record for this book is available from the British Library

Library of Congress Cataloging in Publication Data
Data available

ISBN 0 19 729040 X

Printed by BAS Printers Limited, Over Wallop, Hampshire

THE WISEST HAVE THEIR FOOLS ABOUT THEM

THE MALONE SOCIETY
REPRINTS, VOL. 164
2001

This edition of *The Wisest Have Their Fools About Them*, a hitherto unpublished and untitled play, was prepared by Elizabeth Baldwin and checked by N. W. Bawcutt, G. R. Proudfoot, and H. R. Woudhuysen.

The Society is grateful to Mary, Duchess of Roxburghe, for permission to publish the play, from the unique manuscript, DCR/27/8 Play, in the Cheshire and Chester Archives, and to reproduce pages from it.

April 2001 G. R. PROUDFOOT

INTRODUCTION

The play that is edited here is untitled; it is likewise anonymous. An editorial title of *The Wisest Have Their Fools About Them* has been assigned, based on a proverbial phrase used in the play and the emphasis on the role of the fool in resolving the action. Earlier articles written about the play by the present editor make use of the title *Musophilus*, the name of the principal character. This has, however, been found to cause confusion with the poem *Musophilus* by Samuel Daniel, and wrong assumptions about the play, which the present title is intended to avoid.

The Manuscript

PROVENANCE

Amongst the Crewe family papers in the Cheshire and Chester Archives is a single, untitled, manuscript of a play (DCR/27/8 Play). The text is now kept separately, but was originally in a box (DCR/27/8) of letters, accounts, and deeds, most of which are connected with Sir Ranulph or Randolph Crewe (1558–1646). It is therefore probable that the manuscript came into the family through Sir Ranulph, but in what circumstances can only be guessed at. Sir Ranulph was a member of Lincoln's Inn,[1] and later rose to be Speaker of the House of Commons (1614) and Lord Chief Justice (1625–6). After his removal from office as Lord Chief Justice, he lived a retired life, partly in London and partly in Cheshire. His connection with the Inns of Court and his role in public life would have given him opportunities to acquire the manuscript, although his reasons for doing so remain unclear. He could have been connected in some way with the performance of the play, either as member of the audience, friend of the author, or even butt of some of the jokes.

PHYSICAL DESCRIPTION

The manuscript, which contains only the text of the play edited here, consists of three single leaves, followed by a gathering of six folded folio leaves, all sewn together at the left edge. The sewing is in three irregular sections: at the top are three stitches of grey thread (measured from the top these are at 1–5 mm, 8–23 mm and 38–61 mm); then come five stitches of white thread (at 137–41 mm, 150–61 mm, 171–80 mm, 186–93 mm, and 198–206 mm); finally, ending at the foot, come three further stitches of white thread (at 263–75 mm, 289–300 mm and 307–9 mm). The unevenness of the stitching suggests an unpractised hand. Of the three single leaves, the first

[1] He entered Lincoln's Inn in 1577, was called to the bar in 1584, elected a bencher of Lincoln's Inn in 1600, and an autumn reader in 1602. He became serjeant-at-law in 1615 (*Dictionary of National Biography*, xiii.81).

and second are loose and the third is now completely detached. The leaves measure on average 309 mm × 203 mm and are unnumbered. The area of text varies, with an average of 294 mm × 143 mm; the song on Fol. 11a is inset on both margins. The number of lines on a full page varies from 40 (Fol. 10b) to 54 (Fols. 2a, 2b, and 3b), with text more crowded on the earlier folios. A left-hand column for speech headings is defined by a fold 40 mm from each side of the leaf.

The manuscript is unbound and has suffered damage over the years. The text of the play itself begins on Fol. 1b, and continues to Fol. 15a. The top outer quarter of the first folio has been torn off irregularly and is missing; any title that may have been at the head of the play is therefore lost, except for a few unclear letters in line 1. The lower outer quarter of Fol. 1 is both torn and wrinkled; there is also a tear in the bottom inner quarter of the folio, as well as dirt and staining across the whole of the bottom half. The manuscript has at some point been folded in half, with Fol. 15b to the outside. Fol. 2 also has a tear in the lower outer corner, and there is water staining throughout the manuscript, most heavily in the earlier folios, which are also obscured by dirt in places. On the whole, however, the manuscript is legible and little text has been lost.

A watermark is found in one half of each of the folded sheets, and in two of the three single leaves. The single half-sheets 1*, 2*, 3 are followed by a gathering of six folded sheets: 4*: 15; 5: 14*; 6: 13*; 7*: 12; 8: 11*; and 9*: 10. The asterisks mark the leaves in which the watermarks appear. Fol. 3, which is without a watermark, was probably once conjugate with either Fol. 1 or Fol. 2. The watermark is quite large, and consists of a hand, fingers together and the thumb not visible, with a trefoil or flower at the tip of the index finger (no stem). There is a ruffle at the wrist, with a scalloped cuff covering part of the hand. The cuff is decorated with a central circle and some lines; the ruffle at the wrist is carefully constructed. There is also a trefoil or fleur-de-lis below the wrist, attached to it and pointing down. The watermark is upside down in folios 4, 11, 13, and 14. No exact match to this watermark has been found in either Briquet or Heawood.[2] Neither the detail of the trefoil at the wrist nor other distinctive features, such as the lack of thumb, cuff decoration, and angle of fingers, is found in any recorded watermark. There are some general similarities to Briquet's 11094 (Cologne, 1457), 11144 (various, latest 1547), 11423 (early sixteenth century). Heawood notes that the hand mark 'drops out almost completely after 1600'.[3] However, he mentions, but does not illustrate, examples of the hand watermark from 1614 (with trefoil above) and 1630 (with fleuron above).

[2] C. M. Briquet, *Les Filigranes*, ed. A. Stevenson, 4 vols. (Amsterdam, 1968); Edward Heawood, *Watermarks, Mainly of the 17th and 18th Centuries*, Monumenta Chartæ Papyraceæ Historiam Illustrantia, I (Hilversum, 1950).

[3] Edward Heawood, 'Papers Used in England after 1600. I. The Seventeenth Century to c.1680', 4, *The Library*, 11 (1930–1), 263–99, at p. 283.

The relation to the play itself of writing on Fols. 1a and 15b is unclear. On Fol. 1a, 63 mm from the foot of the page, is a name. This appears to be 'Thomas Mas', though one or two illegible letters may follow the *s*. The page is dirty at this point, and it is not clear whether there are any further letters: it was not possible to examine these notes under ultraviolet light. The handwriting is that of the text and of the notes on Fol. 15b. A line of writing on Fol. 15b appears to be a caption for the folded MS. Written sideways, 135 mm from the left edge and 63 mm from the right, it reads 'Mad in the year of or Lord', followed by what looks like 'La ⟨..⟩ ⟨..⟩'. Also on Fol. 15b, diagonally 33 mm from the top of the page, and on the other half of the folded sheet, is the name 'Thomas'.

LAYOUT OF THE TEXT

The play is divided into five acts with separate scenes. Each scene is headed with its act and scene number, usually in Latin form, though with Arabic numerals. The scribe has sometimes misnumbered the scenes, so that two scenes are headed 'Actus 2dus Scæna 3tia' (296, 338) and the following scenes of Act 2 should accordingly be scenes 5 and 6 rather than 4 and 5. In Act 4, the scribe has skipped a number, so that scene 4 is followed immediately by scene 6, the last in the act. This mistake is probably owing to the fact that scene 4 is particularly long. It also contains the song 'ffond painters love is not a ladd' (952–82; Plate 3), which is set in from both left and right margins, and might, at a casual glance, appear to start a new scene. Verse within prose speeches is also indented from the left (Plate 2).

The left and right margins of the page are generous, although there is little margin at the top or bottom of the page. Speech headings are written in the left margin, usually opposite the first line of the speech in question, except at 236, 385, 652, 723, and 1026, where the speech begins a line (at 385, two lines) before the heading. On occasion they can fall below the line. At 1027 a line is drawn to indicate that the speech heading is misplaced. A line is also drawn to connect speech heading to speech at line 737 (Plate 2). Some headings have been damaged by wear and tear of the manuscript, but only two (24, 155) are lost as a result. In the few instances where a heading is lost or omitted, the sense of the speech usually indicates where a change of speaker is required. It is not clear, however, whether line 510, 'Your knowledge is theoreticall mine practicall', should be spoken by Bond or Musophilus. Line 508 is clearly attributed to Bond, but 509 logically fits Musophilus ('I know not what belongs to law yet I'le try'). Most probable is a rapid change of speakers, from Bond to Musophilus and back to Bond, which the scribe has overlooked. A speech heading for Musophilus has evidently been omitted at line 86. The speech heading is reduplicated at 755 in the left margin as a marker for the marginal addition (Plate 2). A name that is part of the speech is mistaken for a speech heading at 923, but crossed out and the speech begun again with the correct heading. Where a scene involves only one character the speech heading is omitted (1.4, 2.3, 2.'5'[=6], 3.7, 4.2, 5.2), and the initial speech heading is also omitted in 2.1 for Cremulus, who enters with Crusophilus and Genius, and in 3.5 for Fido, who enters before Silly. Speech headings occur in the middle of the line at 142, 444, 1267, and 1303.

Stage directions are generally written either in the scene headings, in the right margin of the text, or at the end of a line of text. A few stage directions are written to the left of the text, among the speech headings (504; 552, Plate 1; 1258), and one entrance is in the middle of a line (541, Plate 1). The directions in the scene headings may, but do not always, name all the characters that appear in the scene, whether or not they enter at the beginning (e.g. 3.3, Plate 1). Additional information as to costume or props is minimal but practical, designed for the stage rather than the study: 'Ente Musophilus in the habit of a waterman and ffido wth him' (49–50), 'Musophilus disguised like a souldier' (339), 'Timothy solus wth a rope' (297), 'Musophilus . Simplicius at severall dores' (233–4), 'Mounsieur Silly, blinded, Musophilus atird lik Cupid' (826–7). Two scenes, 3.6 and 4.1, have no heading; in both cases the speech heading has been set at the left of the second rather than the first line of the opening speech. In 4.1, where there is no space between the scene number and the first line of dialogue, that first line appears to have been added at a later point.

The stage directions in the right margin cover entrances, exits, actions, and manner of performance. They are usually marked off from the rest of the text, either by a single vertical line, or by a more elaborate two- or three-sided box (e.g. 541, Plate 1; 1239–40, Plate 4). In some cases, the box completely surrounds the stage direction (e.g. 205). Stage directions within the text, at the end of the line but not in the margin, are treated similarly. The exit directions are usually in Latin: 'exit, manet vxor' (32), 'exit Cru: Genius manet Cre' (217–19). Some entrances also indicate properties or action: 'enter Cremula an ffido talking together' (392–5), 'enter Moun: wth a paper in his hand' (878–81), 'ent 4 furies and nipp him' (926–7), 'enter Page Vrina, Musophilus and Vrina stand amasd' (1180–4), 'Enter Cru: Ge: Cremulus ledd by his Mayd' (1266–70), 'ente Mu: and Vri: anoints Cre: eyes' (1297–1300). Two entrances (in 3.4 and 3.5) are unmarked, and possibly seven exits, and one entrance may have been lost (106). Four of these are at the end of scenes. Of the others, two involve minor characters leaving the stage on an errand and returning (1.4, 3.3), although in 3.3 the Boy may in fact speak from offstage. In 5.1, Urina must exit after 1075, as Musophilus refers to her absence in his next speech (1076–81). There are also two uses of a singular 'exit' where the plural is required (604, 993).

About twenty-five stage directions deal with necessary action. These are placed in the text where that action should occur, as in 2.3, in which Musophilus, disguised as a soldier, is to pull off Cremulus' spectacles ('takes him by the nose and pulls of his spectacles' (361–3)) and then exit, leaving the spectacles behind ('leave the specacles on the stage' (372–3)). This last direction appears to be imperative, as does that at 1258 ('kneele.'), but all other directions are indicative, so that it may merely be that the final *s* has been omitted in these two instances. The actions indicated in the stage directions are often necessary for later developments of the plot, as with the detailed description surrounding Timothy's attempt to hang himself: 'offers to hang him self and tying the knott of the rope finds a bagg of mony and leaves the rope ther' (317–22). The rope must be left behind so that Cremulus can find it later, when he 'lookes and finds nothing but the rop' (384–6). Other stage directions refer to the manner of performance, as when Cremula (wife of Cremulus and mother of Musophilus) 'makes as if she wept' (160–1). Twice directions of this sort appear in the left margin rather than in the right (504, 1258). The first stipulates that Musophilus 'muses awhile' before responding to Hillarius' question as to his profession, and the second instructs him to kneel when his mother and Fido come on stage in the final scene. Many scenes require few stage directions or none, especially scenes in which a single character enters, addresses the audience, and leaves.

HAND

There are some differences of ink and of letterforms in the manuscript, but these do not suggest the presence of more than one hand at work. As the copying proceeded, there is evidence of diminishing care reflected in a reduction in the number of lines to a page. In folios 1b–8b this varies from 45 (Fol. 6a) to 54 (Fols. 2b, 3b), while the later folios never have more than 50–52 lines to a page (Fols. 11a, 14b), and can have as few as 40 (Fol. 10b). The handwriting is smaller and neater in the earlier folios. From Fol. 12a onwards the ink is paler and browner than on previous leaves, gradually becoming greyer and darker in the following leaves, although never as dark as that of the earlier portion of the manuscript. The marginal addition on Fol. 8b is in a similar grey ink. The lighter, browner ink used from Fol. 12a onwards is also used for corrections throughout the first eight folios of the play, but from line 755 the same ink is used for both main text and corrections.

The play is copied in a single informal and untidy secretary hand with occasional use of italic forms. The writer often retraces letters and words, sometimes merely touching them up. He seems to have corrected the earlier leaves (up to line 755) with ink prepared for writing the second part. The later part of the manuscript is less consistently corrected than the earlier folios, and this, along with the wider spacing of the lines, may indicate that the scribe was pressed for time. The scribe once (Fol. 2a) begins to repeat the last line from the previous page, but deletes it, and once (Fol. 3a) deletes the first line of the page, as if he thought that he had made the same mistake. He then rewrites the line (163). On both these occasions a blank line follows the deletion. He does not make use of catchwords.

The scribe's errors are of the usual type for copyists: dittography, eyeskip, and the omission of letters or words. Lines 294–5, 'ffor though that wanton boyes do mock and flout them/The best and wisest have ther fooles about them' are repeated with minor variation at lines 1157–8, but are there crossed out. The proverb fits the play in either place, and the author may have included it either intentionally or unintentionally, but the scribe, on correcting the MS, may have regarded it as redundant. It is clear that some care has been taken over the corrections: letters or words are deleted eighty-three times, and material has been inserted over sixty times, usually with a caret to indicate where it should come. At line 751, the insertion is too extensive for interlining, and has been written sideways in the margin, with a cross after the line and at the beginning of the insertion to mark where the speech should come (Plate 2). The purpose of the corrections is primarily that the text should make sense. At line 194, 'my' is corrected to 'his' to preserve Cremulus' use of the third person when speaking of himself to his son Crusophilus. This preserves the grammatical accuracy of the sentence, but the inaccuracy is not such that it would have interfered with an audience's understanding of the speech.

A very few lines are missing or incomplete, not counting those affected by damage to the manuscript. Line 695 may be incomplete, although damage makes it difficult to be certain. Line 743 is incomplete, the word 'him' or 'Cupid' being required to complete the sense, but it is also possible that Musophilus interrupts this line. The song at lines 952–82 lacks a final line, required by both sense and rhyme pattern, although again it is possible that Edentula's speech interrupts it. Elsewhere, an interrupted line is indicated by dashes (635). At 608, the scribe has clearly written *hand fort*, but presumably intended the first word as *hang* or *hangd*; at 748 sense and context require M^{rs} where he wrote M^{r}. The worlds *turne over* at 311, which occur nowhere else, would seem to have been copied in error from the exemplar, as they follow the penultimate, rather than the last, line on Fol. 4a. Overall, the corrector has missed few errors: only three instances of dittography, six instances of the omission of words (none of which seriously affects the sense), two omitted speech headings, and the missing words and lines discussed above, remain uncorrected.

The scribe has certain preferences concerning letterforms and spelling. He shows a consistent preference for the italic forms of a few letters; among these are majuscule *H* and *W* and minuscule *f*, *h*, *k*, and *t*. He frequently uses a short *s* in ligatures, especially when the following letter has an ascender, e.g., *h* and *t*. He uses the *æ*, *Æ* digraph throughout in words of Greek and Latin derivation, with only one apparent exception, *Vrinaes* (862), which does not require *æ*, as it is the possessive of *Vrina*. The Greek form of *e* is preferred to the secretary form, but both are used, sometimes in the same word (*free,* 438; *seemd*, 943, Plate 3; *reeding*, 1244, Plate 4), and frequently in the same line. The letters *c* and *t* are very similar, and the scribe seems to have retraced the letter *t* on a number of occasions, especially in the later folios, presumably to make it more distinct from *c*. The bowl of *g* has sometimes been closed with a separate horizontal stroke. The ascender of terminal *d* always slopes steeply to the left (*could*, 1251, Plate 4) and is occasionally flourished with a returning loop (*would*, 758, Plate 2). Majuscule letters are generally preferred at the beginnings of verse lines; the scribe sometimes corrects from minuscule to majuscule, but not all initial minuscules have been corrected. The double *f* form of majuscule *F* is used consistently and is also found in some places where a minuscule would be expected (e.g. *ffar*, 499). The letter *l* is frequently doubled, and the double letters can run together, yielding a triple *l* in *fulll* (476), where a run-together double *l* follows a single *l*. In double *o* the two letters are generally run together. Vowel *u* and consonantal *v* are used medially, but *v* or *V* is used for both initially; *i* is used for both vowel and consonant in both positions, *j* occurring only as a number in scene headings, and possibly for 'I' in one deleted line (54). Some small differences in letterforms on Fol. 13a, where the looping of the letters is slightly looser, could result from the scribe's writing less carefully; they do not seem sufficient to warrant identification of a second hand. Unusual forms of majuscule *M* and *G* occur: the *G* is found in *Gods* (38); a form of majuscule *M* with loops at the bottom is found only on Fol. 13a (1167), but the more usual form is also found there. The initial majuscule of the second word in 554 (Plate 1) has been transcribed without full confidence as a *G*. Further unusual letter forms occur at 263 (*s* in *brokers*), at 502 (*y* in *you*), and 595 (where the *k* in *mistake* may be a compression of *ck*).

SPELLING

The scribe uses several distinctive spellings. The most noticeable include his use of *-ch* for *-tch*, as in *bewich* (976), *bich* (930), *cach* (305, 809), *scrach* (630), *wich* (930). There are no examples of spellings with *-tch*. Although he consistently prefers *ei* spellings to *ie* (e.g. *cheifly* (870)), he reverses this trend with *diety*, used twice (698, 786) to one use of *deity* (528). He frequently omits *e* at the end of words (e.g. *abid* (830), *alik* (563), *hom* (88), *Iudg* (672), *mad* (1118), *min* (386, 804), *Onc*, *onc* (611, 1275), *se* (781)). Most of these words occur with final *e* elsewhere in the text. Omission of *e* also occurs twice in the third person singular of verbs (*chids* (130), *tripudiats* (415)). The scribe shows no clear spelling preference between forms such as *left*/*leaft* (390, 1125/366) and *reeding*/*reading* (882, 1244/342). He seems sometimes to be confused himself over the preferred spelling, as in line 683, where the *y* of *needy* is written over *ie*. In other places he uses *y* despite generally preferring spellings with *ie* (*dy* (609), *ly* (40, 223), *vnty* (83), and even *ny* (281, 708)). Variants which either omit or add a letter (e.g. *sat* (662), *patienly* (789)) are most likely to be the result of scribal error, but there are some which may be genuine variants (*na* (305, 585), *subtile* (955), *volumne* (650)) or, where they occur in speeches by Mounsieur Silly, be intended to reflect the character of his language (*heloquent* (833), *barehead* (836, 837)). Few abbreviations are used: *wth*, *w*th is used frequently, but rarely in compounds (249, 267, 1174). Superscript *M*^{r}, *M*^{rs}, *S*^{r}, *wch*, and *y*^{u} (972–3) are also used. Other abbreviations include *I'l* and *ne'r*. The scribe makes use of tildes over vowels to represent omitted *m* or *n* (*hī*, 552, Plate 1). At 762 the nonsense word *granham* has a horizontal line above *anha* which can hardly be construed as a mark of abbreviation and whose function accordingly remains unclear. Act and scene numbers are regularly abbreviated as a Roman or Arabic number followed by an appropriate ending, such as *jus*, 2da, and so on. A *par* abbreviation is required by the sense of lines 857 (*pted*), 33, 81, 155, 1223, and 1326 (*pt*), but the form of the first letter appears to be identical to that of *p* used elsewhere. The hand, the types and number of errors, and to some extent the variation of spelling, point to a copyist, working in some haste, who nevertheless had time to go over the manuscript and correct errors. The nature of his errors makes it unlikely that he was the author.

The Play

DATE

Although evidence for the date of the play is inconclusive, its cumulative weight suggests a date in the 1620s, and probably in the later years of that decade. Topical allusions within the play are often so general that they could have been made long after the events they refer to, as is the case with the reference to Banks's horse (1251). It may be that there are also more specific 'in-jokes', understood only by the author, actors, and original audience. It is tempting, for instance, to speculate, as the play was apparently once in the possession of Sir Ranulph Crewe, that the line 'let the silver thredds of your golden compassion bind vp the decayed wants of a poore souldier' (348–50) may contain a reference to Crewe's prosecution of Sir Francis Mitchell for alleged corrupt practices in executing 'the commission concerning gold and silver thread' in 1616.[4] If one could make this connection, it would imply a very specific audience, with a substantial number of lawyers and courtiers in it, who would remember the case. But it is not necessary for an understanding of the play that the line should have a hidden meaning, and it may indeed have nothing to do with either Crewe or Mitchell.

Both the handwriting of the manuscript and the events in the life of Sir Ranulph Crewe, the putative original owner, are in keeping with a date in the 1620s. The hand is from the first half of the seventeenth century and, given the play's subject matter and London setting, it probably came into Sir Ranulph's possession during or shortly after the time that he was a public figure in London. Sir Ranulph was particularly active in parliamentary, court, and legal circles between 1614 and 1626, after which little more is heard of him, although he still sometimes visited London and presumably stayed in touch with friends and acquaintances there.

The 'Devill in St Dunstones' (333), at which Timothy plans to carouse, was the Devil and St Dunstan in Fleet Street, home of Jonson's Apollo Club. The inn is first mentioned in 1609, when Simon Wadlow appeared in a list of licensed vintners. Jonson's involvement with the inn seems to have been

[4] *DNB*, xiii.81.

largely after 1616, and Wadlow died in 1627, although the business was carried on by his widow and son.[5] The play is therefore likely to date from later than 1609, as the inn would not have been immediately famous.

The names of several characters are found in printed plays of the period.[6] The name Chremylos ('man of property'; formed from the root *chrema*, 'property') and the fact of his having a wife originate in the *Ploutos* of Aristophanes. On the English stage, the protagonist, Crobolus, of Edward Forsett's Latin play *Pedantius*, 1581, is described in its argument as a onetime servant of Chremulus. Chremyla is the name given by Thomas Randolph to the anonymous wife of his Chremylus in *Ploutophthalmia Ploutogamia; or, Hey for Honesty, Down with Knavery*, a free version of the *Ploutos*, performed at Trinity College, Cambridge, *c.*1626–8, and printed in a revised version in 1651. There is a Fido in Jonson's *Every Man Out of his Humour*, 1600, a Chrysophilus ('lover of gold') in Edmund Stub's *Fraus Honesta*, 1619, a Simplicius in Marston's *What You Will*, 1601, and Randolph's *Cornelianium Dolium*, 1638, and a Silly in Jonson's *The New Inn*, 1629. Bobadilla is used of male characters in Jonson's *Every Man In his Humour*, 1598, and Beaumont and Fletcher's *Love's Cure*, 1606. Timothy is frequent, as is Medea, while Lais is a stock name for a courtesan. Musophilus ('lover of the Muse(s)'), occurs in no printed play but is the title of a poem by Samuel Daniel, *Musophilus: containing a general defence of learning* (1611; first printed in 1599, and reprinted three times with revisions by 1611). Other names not found in printed plays of the period are: Hilarius (though James Shirley uses the name Hilaria in *The School of Compliment*, 1625, and Massinger Hilario in *The Picture*, 1629), Bebia, Pretty, Urina, Edentula (='toothless', see line 983), Sill, and Trulla. These parallels, and the possible relation of the play to Randolph's version of Aristophanes, seem consistent with a dating in the late 1620s. The action of the present play may even contain, in the cure of blind Cremulus, a parodic echo of the cure of Ploutos, the blind god of wealth, by Asclepios, god of medicine, in the *Ploutos*. The agent of Cremulus' cure, Mrs Urina, is not divine; Randolph, indulging in a stock English joke against doctors, has the servant Carion twice refer to Esculapius as a 'Urinal' (sigs. $D4^{v}$, $F4^{r}$).

An intriguing, but uncertain, connection can be suggested between the plot of the play and a line in a verse elegy formerly attributed to John Donne, 'A Tale of a Citizen and his Wife'. In the poem, the reaction of a character is compared to that of one who has hidden gold but, returning, found only a rope: 'Looke how hee look'd that hid the gold (his hope)/And at returne found nothing but a Rope'.[7] This exactly describes the situation in the play

[5] Jacob Henry Burn, *A Descriptive Catalogue of the London Traders, Tavern, and Coffee-House Tokens Current in the Seventeenth Century, Printed for the Use of the Members of the Corporation of the City of London* (London, 1853), pp. 75–81.

[6] T. L. Berger, W. C. Bradford, and S. L. Sondergard, *An Index of Characters in Early Modern English Drama: Printed Plays, 1500–1660* (Cambridge, 1998).

[7] John Donne, *The Elegies and The Songs and Sonnets*, ed. Helen Gardner (Oxford, 1965), 'A Tale of a Citizen and his Wife', lines 64–5.

(2.4): the usurer Cremulus has hidden a bag of money given him by his elder son, Crusophilus; this money is then discovered by Timothy (debtor to Cremulus) as he is preparing to hang himself. He takes the money and leaves the rope, which is then discovered by Cremulus, looking for his gold. Cremulus in turn attempts to hang himself. Helen Gardner traces the source of this story to the *Greek Anthology*, ix.44: 'A man finding gold left his halter, but the man who had left the gold and did not find it, hanged himself with the halter he found.'[8] Topical references in the poem date it to 1609.[9] The classical source for this story may indicate only that the playwright was a man of education, but it may also be a reference shared by the playwright and his audience. Donne certainly expects his audience to be familiar with the story. The story also survives in a Latin version by Ausonius (Epigrams 14) and an English one by Sir Thomas Wyatt (Tottel's *Songs and Sonnets* (1557), sig. K4r ['Kiii']).

Identifiable borrowings are hard to locate because the playwright was clearly familiar with a good many plays of the period, or at least with their general stock of ideas and characters. There may be allusions to the works of other dramatists. Some parallels exist in language and expression, in characters and character names, and even in situation, between the plays of Jonson and the present text, but many of these can be seen as belonging to the common stock. Many phrases in the play, although not strictly proverbial, are probably common sayings or popular expressions, such as 'the towns our owne' (798), which occurs in two of Jonson's entertainments (*Pan's Anniversary* (1620), 85–6 and *Neptune's Triumph* (1624), 522), as well as in Cavendish's *The Country Captain* (558). References to the Devil and St Dunstan tavern are found in a number of plays. The framing of laws by Timothy in the tavern scene, and the scene itself, could allude to Jonson's Apollo Club, but it may be referred to merely as a well-known pub. More interesting is the number of times that Jonson includes Cupid as a character in his masques. The episode in 4.3 in which Mounsieur Silly seeks to meet Cupid reflects these conventions. Silly, as a courtier, has seen Cupid on the stage, but is unable to distinguish between fiction and reality. Comparison with other plays reveals no clear evidence of direct borrowing, but shows that the same themes, proverbial phrases, stock characters and occasionally jokes are being used. For instance, Shakespeare's *The Comedy of Errors* (intended for performance at Gray's Inn in 1594, printed 1623) contains comic business with a rope and a bag of gold, and a line from it 'My youngest boy, and yet my eldest care' (I. 1. 124) may be echoed at lines 10, 'my youngest sonne', and 16, 'eldest care'. Similarly, Silly's plagiarism may recall that of Matheo/Matthew in Jonson's *Every Man In his Humour* (1601 and 1616).

The following are examples of phrases used in both *The Wisest Have Their Fools About Them* and some of the works of Ben Jonson.

[8] Gardner, p. 229. [9] Ibid., p. 227.

182–3: 'I love not fetters though composd of gold' (proverbial, Tilley M338[10])

Jonson,[11] *Eastward Ho!* (1605), IV. ii. 151–2: 'no man loues his fetters, be they made of gold.'

266–7: 'if not I'l make the Deane of Dunstable and that gratis too wthout any simonie'

Jonson, *The Gyspies Metamorphosed* (1621), 1286–7: 'Spight o' the Constable,/Or deane of Dunstable.'
(Dunstable is in Bedfordshire, where the Duke of Buckingham had property, and the reference in Jonson may be local, whereas that in *The Wisest* may be a pun on the proverbial stupidity of the men of Dunstable (Tilley D646); however, the suggestion of simony may be a dig at the practice of selling appointments, in which Buckingham was involved.)

267–8: 'or sirra dost thou heare thou shalt be a Iud,ge canst thou sleep well vpon a bench,'

Jonson, *The Gypsies Metamorphosed* (1621), 719–22: 'He'is a sight that will take/An old Iudg from his wenche,/I, and keepe him awake,/Yes, awake o' the benche.'

568–70: 'Weele make a Law that whosever ⟨af⟩te^{r} they have drunk ther full cupp do not sweeten ther mouths wth a kisse shall drink double,'

Jonson, *The New Inn* (1631), I. vi. 79: 'Or kiss, or drink afore me'
(This is glossed as meaning 'you have taken the words out of my mouth', but it may have reference to the kiss-and-drink game.)

612: 'Els let me never see more goulden shower.' (possibly also proverbial, or a reference to the story of Jupiter and Danae)

Jonson, *Eastward Ho!* (1605), V. i. 97–9: 'nowe I remember my Song o' the *Golden Showre*, why may not I haue such a fortune?'

771–2: 'This mans toung is a gentle man vsher it goe before his witt.'

Jonson, *Poetaster* (1601), IV. v. 143–4: 'His tongue shall bee gent'man vsher to his wit, and still goe before it.'
(In both instances, the playwright plays on the proverb (Tilley T412) of the tongue running before the wit, and on a gentleman usher going before his employer.)

In addition, Musophilus' disguising as Cupid in 4.3 to deceive the blindfolded Mounsieur Silly probably derives from Jonson's *The Alchemist*, III. v, in which Dol, disguised as the Fairy Queen, appears to the blindfolded Dapper. The pinching of Dapper by fairies in this scene is transferred to the pinching of Mounsieur Silly by furies in 4. 4.

The plot of the play hinges on the ability of Musophilus to get the court

[10] Morris Palmer Tilley, *A Dictionary of the Proverbs in England in the Sixteenth and Seventeenth Centuries: A Collection of the Proverbs Found in English Literature and the Dictionaries of the Period* (Ann Arbor, Mich., 1950).

[11] Quotations are taken from *Ben Jonson*, ed. C. H. Herford, Percy and Evelyn Simpson, 11 vols. (Oxford, 1925–52).

fool, Simplicius, to obtain a grant to him of the lands given to his brother Crusophilus by the expedient of 'begging him for a fool', that is, having Crusophilus declared incompetent to handle his affairs. This alludes to the practice of obtaining writs *de idiota inquirendo*, by which the king was able to grant to any of his subjects the profits of the lands (as well as custody of the person) of anyone proven mentally incompetent.[12] This practice was evidently abused in some cases but was clearly well known, as witness allusions to it in other plays, and became proverbial (Tilley F496).[13] The device of having the fool beg the fool evidently amuses the court and so ensures the success of the petition; the practice was not unknown offstage, as can be seen by the role played by James I's fool, Archy Armstrong, who by 1618 was 'so influential, that he was used as intermediary for the presentation of petitions to the King'.[14] Enid Welsford suggests that the presence of court-fools in plays written between 1619 and 1624 'may possibly be due to the growing fame of the royal jester Archy Armstrong'.[15]

Cremulus' wish in 2.1, that 'mony may fall to five ith hundred' (226–7) if he allows Timothy any more time to pay his debt may contain a reference to the Act against Usury of 1623–4, which mentions an interest rate of up to 10 per cent, and forbids more than 8 per cent after 24 June 1625. This Act was to continue for seven years, and Cremulus might envisage a further fall in interest rates.[16]

There is one final conjectural piece of evidence concerning date. In 3.6, the second Soldier claims that the soldiers 'have bine wher we have done service for the common wealth, In sat Ilands', to which Musophilus replies, 'I'm sure the salt of Sapience hath forsaken the powdering tubs of your braines' (661–4). Given that Musophilus' reply is probably punning, it seems likely that the islands in question are the Salt Islands, rather than the unlocatable Sat Islands. The likeliest candidates for the Salt Islands are at La Rochelle, which not only produced and exported salt at the time but was the object of an English military campaign. The campaign was beset with funding difficulties from the beginning, and was overall a disaster. The English made an initial landing in Île de Ré, which contains extensive salt marshes, in July 1627. The campaign was a catalogue of unsuccessful attacks, inadequate reinforcements, starvation, and disease. The assassination of Buckingham on 23 August 1628 did not immediately end the campaign, but removed its most energetic supporter. The begging Soldiers' claim to have received no pay would certainly ring true in 1627–8; both soldiers and sailors in London and Portsmouth, waiting to embark for La Rochelle, were

[12] Enid Welsford, *The Fool: His Social and Literary History* (New York, 1961), p. 160.

[13] Middleton and Rowley make an allusion to it in *The Changeling* (ed. George Walton Williams (London, 1967), IV. iii. 205–6, note), and both Shakespeare (*Com. Err.* II. i. 41) and Jonson (*Every Man Out of his Humour*, III. v. 13) show that they were aware of the practice.

[14] Welsford, p. 174; she refers to the *State Papers Domestic* James I, vol. xcviii, no. 89, as evidence of this practice. Cf. also *OED*, beg, *v.* 5a.

[15] Welsford, pp. 248–9.

[16] 21 James I c.17.

unpaid or inadequately paid, and riots occurred. Buckingham was the focus of blame, and his house was besieged by hungry sailors.[17] Musophilus' reference to 'a Duke that keepes open house' (683–4) may suggest Buckingham. The ducal residence he refers to is, however, the tomb of Sir John Beaumont, known as 'Duke Humphrey's tomb' on the south side of the nave of St Paul's cathedral.[18] Contemporary allusions to Duke Humphrey's tomb in connection with servants looking for work, as well as ex-soldiers, hangers-on, petty confidence tricksters, and other opportunists looking for a meal are frequent.[19] 'Dining with Duke Humphrey' became proverbial for going hungry (Tilley D637).

Some of the words used in the text are first cited in the *Oxford English Dictionary* in the 1620s and 1630s, supporting other evidence for a date around the late 1620s or early 1630s. These words include *æquality* (1228) (1635), *angust* (334) (1599, but used in Burton's *Anatomy of Melancholy* in 1621), *barehead* (836) (1622, but the application in the play is unusual), *bespedd* (42) (*c*.1630), *captivated* (731) (1621), *combustible* (1192) (in sense of 'easily kindled to violence or passion', 1647; in sense 'burning, fiery', 1632; the usage in the play tends to the former sense), *corporeall* (1191) (in sense 'material', 1622), *croane* (417) ('rarely applied to a worn-out old man', 1630), *cutt out* (100) (1645), *eclipsed* (706) (in sense 'suffering from eclipse, darkened', 1633), *epitomise* (335) (in sense 'to summarize, to give a concise account of; to state the essence of a matter briefly', 1624), *excrementitious* (1015) (1636, but also in sense of 'the dregs or worthless part of any substance', 1623), *ingenuous* (498) (1598, but in sense 'of free or honourable birth' 1638), *plaudits* (238) (1624), *practicall* (510) (in sense 'relating to practice rather than theory', 1617), *suspension* (432) (1635), *theoreticall* (510) (in sense 'relating to theory, rather than practice', 1652; in sense of 'contemplative', 1623), *tick tock* (133, 1160) (the play's usage antedates the *OED* date of 1848 and offers the unrecorded sense of knocking at a door), and *tripudiats* (415) (1623). The word *medioxiniall* (1069), which refers to gods of the middle order, does not appear in the *OED*, although words of similar sense are cited in the late seventeenth and early eighteenth century (*medioxumous*, 1664; *medioxumate*, 1723).

AUTHOR

Although the names 'Thomas Mas' and 'Thomas' are written on the Fols. 1a and 15b of the play text, it is not clear that they relate to the authorship of

[17] Marcel Delafosse, *Histoire de la Rochelle* (Toulouse, 1985), pp. 117, 149; Roger Lockyer, *Buckingham: the Life and Political Career of George Villiers, 1st Duke of Buckingham, 1592–1628* (London and New York, 1981), pp. 381–404. I am grateful to Professor Alan Nelson for suggesting the connection with La Rochelle.

[18] Thomas Nashe, *Works*, ed. R. B. McKerrow, rev. F. P. Wilson, 5 vols. (Oxford, 1958), 4.93, note on 1, 163, 23–4.

[19] W. Sparrow Simpson, *Gleanings from Old St. Paul's* (London, 1889), pp. 268–9, 275–7; W. Sparrow Simpson, *St. Paul's Cathedral and Old City Life* (London, 1894), p. 194.

the play. The name(s) may indicate authorship, but could equally well indicate ownership of the manuscript or participation in a performance. 'Mas' might be part of Massey, a common Cheshire name, but no Thomas Massey is on record in connection with either of the universities or the Inns of Court at this time, nor does any of the Thomas Masseys listed as having wills proved in Cheshire in the period seem likely.

The author's familiarity with many plays of the period, perhaps particularly those of Ben Jonson, and also perhaps with Jonson's connection with the Devil and St Dunstan tavern has already been illustrated. He also had some idea of how a play needed to work on stage; there are weaknesses in the plot, but the play is clearly designed for performance, and has both pace and structure. If the author was part of, or on the fringes of, the Jonson circle, he may well have expected his audience to pick up the allusions to Jonson's plays, and to Jonson's favourite tavern. Personal jokes, if indeed there are any, are lost to us, or at most can only be guessed at. At an early performance, they could have been the key to the play's success, just as topical jokes about university figures in an undergraduate revue depend on the audience's knowledge of the personalities involved.

The playwright evidently knew some Latin and Greek, and expected his audience to share this knowledge. As previously noted, the names of several characters are of Greek origin, and lines 595–8 contain puns in Latin. The Latin is predominantly law Latin, and occurs in one of the scenes involving the lawyer Hilarius and his clerk Bond (3.4). In addition, both Musophilus and, to an even greater extent, Timothy, use Latinate words, such as *angust* (334, 'straight, narrow, compressed'), *exuperatt*, (421, 'to overtop, surpass, excel; to overcome') *medioxiniall* (1069), and *tripudiats* (415, *OED* 'to dance for joy, or with excitement; to exult'). The scribe's *I no triumphe* (798) may result from his misunderstanding of the Latin *Io, triumphe*, or the error may be Mounsieur Silly's. The *Ploutos* of Aristophanes, in the original or in Randolph's English version, and the Greek original of the episode of the hiding of a bag of gold and finding of a rope may have been known to some in the audience, but knowledge of neither is needed in order to follow the play.

PERFORMANCE AND CONTEXT

Although it is clear from the structure of the play and the care taken with the stage directions that the original was intended, and even prepared, for performance, there is no evidence as to whether or not it was in fact performed, nor of the purpose for which the surviving copy was made. If the surviving text was intended as only a reading transcript for an admirer of the show, the copyist has been very careful about preserving and correctly placing stage directions, but not careful enough to produce an elegant copy. The surviving transcript could equally well be used by a troupe of players to give a performance. The addresses and references to the audience by characters (principally Musophilus and Simplicius) further indicate an envisaged performance. They may also give some indication of the context of such a performance. The connection with Ranulph Crewe might suggest that this is an Inns of Court play. The final few lines of the play (1328–33) are similarly suggestive: Musophilus invites the cast to his wedding, saying

> Thus to the Church we'el go when thou art there
> Then t'is a Temple I durst bouldly swear
> Wee'le all be merry, and our noblest guest
> Will take ther welcome for ther greatest feast
> I would say mor but that for this perhapp
> The author sayth he feares an after clappe.

The primary sense is that the church will become a temple dedicated to Urina (cf. line 1061, where Urina is described as 'a Temple vowd to purity'); in an Inns of Court context, it would carry a secondary allusion either to the Inner or Middle Temple. The feast could in that case refer to the occasion of the performance. Earlier (1096–1100), Musophilus makes a direct address to the audience:

> I thought what my round capp and my sophisticall
> gowne would come too, all you that be present,
> courtiers or what degree so ever [⟨you..y⟩ of] studdie ,studdie,
> hard, to be fooles, that you may wth the more facility
> inherit your ffathers lands,

The phrase 'courtiers or what degree so ever' may of course be flattery of the audience, but it is more likely that it indicates that some, at least, of the audience might be of the degree of courtier and that all might aspire to legal knowledge in the hope of inheriting landed property.

A more general reference in an exchange between Simplicius and Musophilus makes use of the trick of compelling the audience to laugh by attributing a disreputable cause to failure to do so. Simplicius asks Musophilus, who he has heard can 'coniure', to tell who 'loves a wench best of all this companie', to which Musophilus replies that 'Banks his horse could doe that, I'l tell the all the spectators especialy those that doe not laugh they that look as though butter would not melt in ther mouths' (1247–54). Such a joke might best succeed with an audience containing some members of greater gravity than others, particularly if they were also of higher status. A private rather than a public performance is more likely to involve an audience of mixed ages and dignities, comprising a group who know each other sufficiently well to detect personal allusions in topical jokes.

Any connection with the Inns of Court, however, must remain putative. The association of the manuscript with the Crewe family only shows ownership and is far from conclusive as evidence for its provenance. The play could as well fit a university context as a legal one, or that of a civic banquet, or even that of court performance, although at this date city and court festivities were less likely to involve such a dramatic entertainment.

The structure of the play allows twenty-seven characters to be played by eight or nine performers, three of them boys for the female roles. This is a feasible number for a professional troupe.[20] The stage directions are clear at those points where clarity is needed to explain the action on the stage, as when first Timothy (317–22) and later Cremulus (396–8) try to hang themselves, or when Musophilus pulls off Cremulus' spectacles (361–3). Although the author need not have been professional, he certainly shows a familiarity with the stage and the necessities of professional performance and may have envisaged performance by professionals.

The play's requirements for set and properties are neither extensive nor difficult. There needs to be a 'house' with a door, representing first Cremulus' and later Urina's house, at which Musophilus can twice knock (133, 1160). Cremulus' house may have an inner area, as Cremula is addressed as being 'within' (21). It is also important that there be a beam on which Cremulus can hide his bag of money (222–4), and which Timothy can use to tie the rope with which he plans to hang himself before he finds the money (317–22). A rope and a bag of money are needed for this scene (2.3), and, as money is exchanged several times, smaller moneybags or purses are also required. Cremulus wears spectacles, specifically mentioned in the stage directions, which are pulled off by Musophilus (361–3). There is what amounts to a running joke about Cremulus' spectacles, and although they are necessary to the plot (his ultimate blindness is crucial for the final cure and reconciliation), it is possible that there is also a personal allusion to some member of the audience.

Other properties include a bag, carried by Bond, which Musophilus assumes contains money (515). Several characters (Cremulus (1.1), Musophilus (4.1), Silly, Urina (4.4)) at some point have letters or papers that they read, find, or give to someone else. The same paper, of course, could be used more than once. Silly also may be writing, or pretending to write, in the scene in which he composes verses to Cupid (3.5). Drinking vessels are needed in two scenes (1.2, 3.3), particularly the tavern scene (3.3). Finally, a container of liquid or something with which Urina can anoint Cremulus' eyes is needed for the final scene (5.5).

Costumes too are simple. Musophilus must change costume several times: he is 'in the habit of a waterman' (49) at his first appearance, and later disguises himself as a soldier to beg from his father (2.3). He disguises himself as Cupid to fool Mounsieur Silly, whom he beats (849–51) with a stick (perhaps a slapstick). Otherwise he is presumably dressed as a scholar, as his reference to 'my round capp and my sophisticall gowne' (1096–7) suggests. The costumes of the other characters are not specified, although the four soldiers probably require distinctive costumes, and the four furies must surely have been masked, especially if they are being doubled by other

[20] For a discussion of the possible combinations of parts, see Elizabeth Baldwin, '*Musophilus*: A Newly-Discovered Seventeenth-Century Play', in *Essays in Honour of Peter Meredith*, Leeds Studies in English 29 (Leeds, 1998), pp. 35–47.

members of the company. They too would be distinctively costumed.

Editorial Conventions

The following conventions are used in this edition. Square brackets enclose deleted material, and also folio numbers. Angle brackets indicate text lost or made difficult or impossible to decipher by damage to the manuscript; dots within angle brackets stand for the illegible or lost characters (⟨..⟩).

Line numbering is continuous for the text of the play, including cancelled lines, headings, and (where they occupy a separate line) stage directions. Interlineations are lowered into the text, and noted in the textual footnotes; carets are not printed, but their presence is recorded. The position of elements of the text such as speech-prefixes, stage directions, headings, and indentations is reproduced as exactly as type permits; slight misalignments are ignored. On two occasions (709, 779) an exceptionally long line has spread into two lines of print.

Superscript letters have been printed in the same size of type as the remainder of the text; not all abbreviations have fully suspended letters, and this is represented as exactly as possible in the text. The positioning of punctuation above or below the line has been normalized. Unusual duplication or spacing of marks of punctuation have, as far as possible, been retained. The scribe's practice frequently makes it difficult to distinguish his full stops from his commas.

The editor and the Society wish to thank the staff of the Cheshire and Chester Archives for their support and assistance throughout and for supplying the photographs of the passages reproduced in the Plates.

List of Characters

in order of appearance

Cremulus, a Usurer
Cremula, his wife
Musophilus, his younger son, a poor student
Fido, friend of Musophilus
Timothy, Cremulus' neighbour, in debt to him
Unice, Cremulus' maid
Crusophilus, elder son of Cremulus, a fool
Genius, associate of Crusophilus
Simplicius, the Court Fool
Hilarius, a Lawyer
Bond, Hilarius' clerk
Monsieur Carouse, Timothy's drinking companion
Lais, Bebia } women at the tavern
A Boy, Drawer at the tavern
Pretty, Hilarius' maid
Mounsieur Silly, a Gentleman Usher, aspring to be a Courtier
4 Soldiers, beggars
Mistress Urina, a Physician's daughter
Bobadilla, a young woman, associate of Urina
Edentula, an old woman, associate of Urina
4 Furies, called Medaea, Menippa, Sill, and Trulla
A Singer (4.4)
A Page, at Urina's house
Cremulus' Maid, perhaps Unice

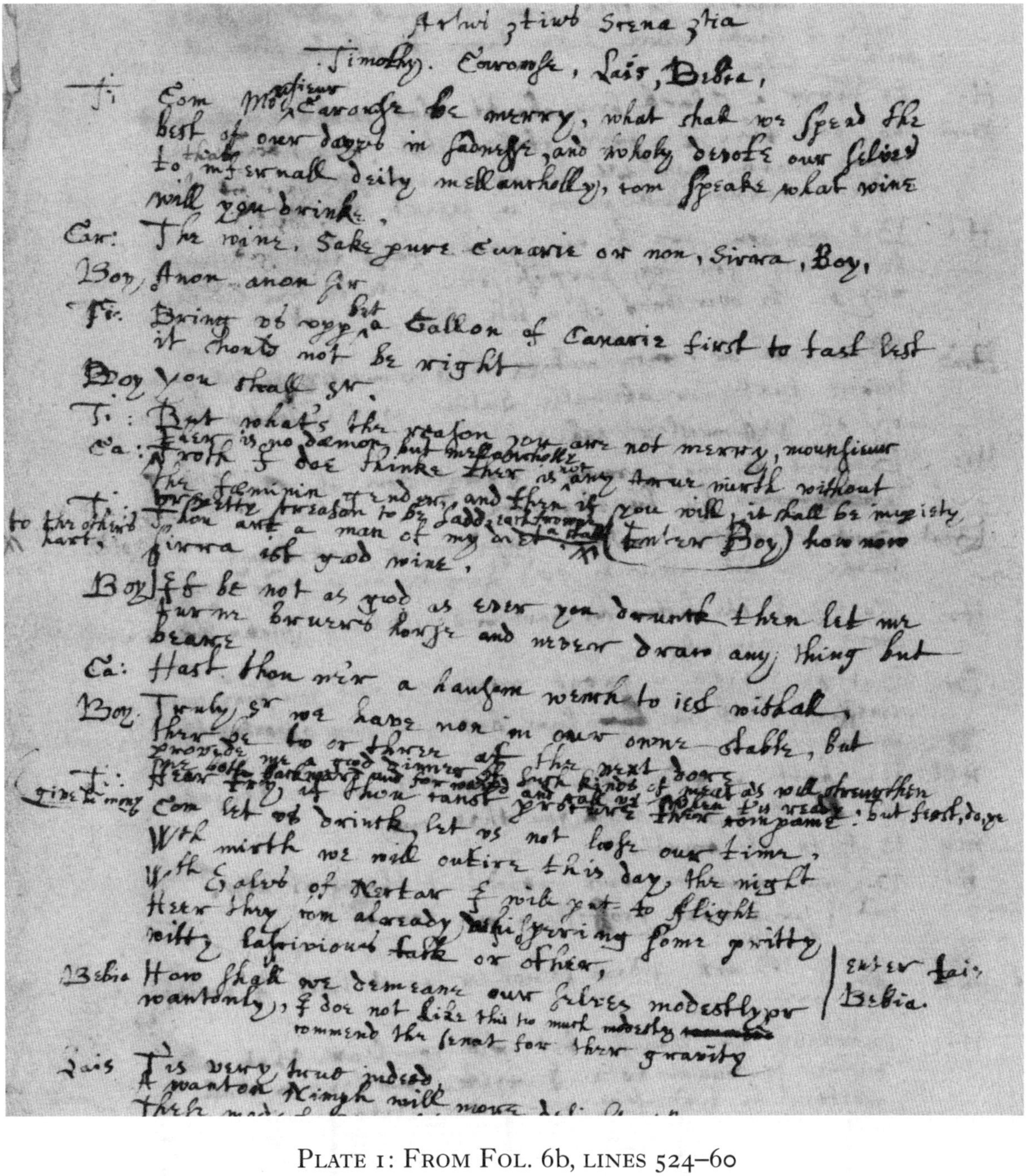

PLATE I: FROM FOL. 6b, LINES 524–60

character wherby you may easly know him therfore
Il leave you exit.

Mu: I long to see my purchase, I must be altogether
Cupidate and speak nothing vnder the straine of
a Lover, here he comes serrato by the passions of
Omnipotent Cupid and captivated by his predominancie
This same is he whose mouth spits flaming fire
Whose heart like Ætna burnes wth love desire

enter Mounsier—

Moun: Over head eares in woefull love
Now Cupid for thy mother dove
help help helpe.

Mu: —O most kind most curteous Cupid

Moun: What's that you say of Cupid you are not acquainted wth
him I pray sir are you,

Mu: I would not for more then I speak of loose that
interest I have in him

Moun: I will give all my estat for on halfe howers
acquaintance wth

Mus: Let me feel your pulse, you are deeply in love, but
can you tell the mrs of your affections

Moun: troth there are so many pritty soules I know
not wch to affect most.

Mu: There is a Phisitians Daughter on Mrs Urina
her very name will make your mouth water

Moun: Mak water in my mouth, O mrs Urina, I but
will you cast forth a good word for me

Mus: Me: I tell the I'l make her all to belove the, she
shall never rest till shee meet the heere, but first
arme the wth some potent magick charmes

Moun: What be they my chaps would faine be champing
them

Mu: I I'l doe as many a rurall chaplaine
mak divinity all rhethorick for
your lordship

PLATE 2: FROM FOL. 8b, LINES 726–59

Bobo: Tis very strange that iust as we were talking of
love this outragious lover should come in.

Pri: And sure his mind wth strong affections tainted
lookt through his eyes as through a glasse that's painted

Eron: And that to love their beuties never movd him
But therefore beuties second because she lovd him.
I think in conscience I was as hansom as either of
both these when I was a young wench, oh I was
as plumpe as the grape, O happy who that got the
first breach of my maydenhead, that was as I remember
twixt foure and five yeares of age, but now I must
confesse I am growne an auncient bearer.

Pri: Heer be the countiers verses Ile read these when I have
more leisure, but hark what musicks this, Love sings

Fond painters love is not a ladd
Wth bow and shafts and feathers cladd
Much sawer is he felt than seen
His substance subtile slight and thinne
Oft leapes he from the glauncing eyes
Oft in the snowy mounts he lyes
Oft lurks he twixt the ruddy lipps
Thence while the heart his Nectar sipps
Oft in a voice creepes downe the eare
Oft hides his darts in goulden haire
Oft blushing cheeks do light his fires
Oft in a smooth soft skin retires
Often in smiles often in teares
His flaming heat in water beares
When nothing els kindles desire
Even vertues selfe shall blow the fire
Love wth a thousand darts abounds
— Surest and deepest vertue wounds
Oft times …

PLATE 3: FROM FOL. 11a, LINES 938–69

Cre: Witt without mony is lik a bagg puddin without fatt
com let vs trye if we can find Musophilus, in him
we will repeat the second lesson of our patience. exeunt

Actus 3tus Scena 3ta

Musophilus Simplicius

Mu: I wonder Simplicius stays so long it makes me
suspect the event, surely he hath not wit enough to prove
disloyall, heer he comes, wth a cheerefull looke as if Enter Sim:
he din successfull, now noble Simplicius have you
speddo,

Sim: Doe you make a question of it, heer it is in black
and white, full power and authority to take possession
of all that you can call his, they laught at the reading
of the articles, heer take, it I must leave you
for I have a suit, of mine owne to ffollowe, but Sirra
dost heare I heard say thou canst coniure,

Mu: I have studdied the black art

Sim: The Divell you have, but can you tell me who
loves a wench best of all this companie,

Mu: Bankes his horse could doe that, Il tell the all
the spectators especialy those that doe not laugh
they that look as though butter would not melt
in their mouths

Sim: Adieu madd wagg remember my speech. exit

Mus: Well, now I am at the height of my wishes, heare
must my hopes be terminated, nor could I wish
a greater happinesse, heer comes a paire of the Enter
truest friends that ever my bosome harboured, now shall Cremula
I be forgetfull of my duty and your curtesie ffi:

Cre: How my wretched Musophilus

Mu: Who, wretched

Plate 4: From Fol. 14a, lines 1231–62

[Fol. 1a blank except for name 'Thomas Mas']

[Fol. 1b]

...⟩⟨i⟩f⟨i⟩ ,
...⟩a ja
...⟩wth a letter in his
...⟩pectacles on his nose

...⟩me wth letters nay and
...h⟩ese his Academicall
...⟩hipwrack of youth
...⟩e a story of sciences
...⟩rall sciences, is this
...⟩ is my youngest sonne
...⟩ce, [let him] ⟨...⟩ths since he went to travell., let him goe and live by his
...⟩nd an Indian mine, ther
..⟩ ⟨C⟩ram his pockets, replenish
...⟩should want roome enough,
..⟩ ⟨s⟩top his mouth wth gould
...⟩eldest care, My sonne
...⟩ ⟨b⟩etter mould, his meanes
...⟩ encreaseth dayly.
...⟩ ⟨i⟩nto my store,
⟨.o⟩ ⟨...⟩⟨s⟩ire the more.
...⟩within ther Cremula, was not my
...⟩ Timothy heere, to repay my principle
...⟩my vse. — enter Cremula
...⟩ No not yet.
⟨C⟩remulus O false periurd slave, well he hath forfeted his
bond his land is morgagd , a dainty fine seat all's
mine owne 'Tis mony, mony, keepes the world in awe
Whatso'ere getts coine, that only is my law
Cremula. But I pray what is that in your hand

Fol. 1 top outer quarter missing 6 *...h⟩ese*] ascender of *h* visible before *e* 9 *sciences,*] comma added later 11 *[let him]*] blot over deletion *⟨...⟩ths ... and*] interlined above deletion with caret *let him goe and*] in paler ink 13 *replenish*] *sh* altered from earlier *sh* 14 *roome*] smudge above (but not obscuring) *e* 17 *⟨b⟩etter*] *b* conjectural; ascender and part of body visible 18 *⟨...⟩ encreaseth*] *n* damaged 19 *⟨i⟩nto*] further minim partially visible before *n* 20 *⟨s⟩ire*] descender of long *s* visible before *i* 21 *within*] top of *wit* torn off *Cremula*] tear from *C* of *Cremula* down nine lines to *e* of *sonne* in line 30; *C* is split in half 22 *...⟩*] remains of a letter, possibly *r*, visible at edge of page (torn) *to*] *t* split in half by tear 24 *No*] *N* torn 25 *⟨C⟩remulus*] edge of *C* visible before *r* *well*] *e* mostly obliterated by tear 26 *morgagd ,*] tear between *d* and comma, but comma not written directly after *d* 29 *Cremula*] only one minim of *u* visible

Cremulus A petition from your sonne Musophilus
Crēula A⟨n⟩d will you not graunt him his request
Crēulus As much love as you will but no mony.(exit, manet vxor)
Cremula. Poore love when you will pt wth a litle of your dust to
releive his necessity, No not by my entreaty, he prefers
his wealth before wife or child, married, now heaven
defend if this be marriage, thus to be griped in the
pawes of such an vsurer and bedded in his bowells
O all ye Nuptiall Gods why was I bound [t.]
To this vncha⟨r⟩itable peece of man
His life and mirth doth in his coffers ly
⟨Curst⟩ be that ceremoniall ring wch d⟨i⟩d vs ioine
⟨Cur⟩st be that day when first I was bespedd
Curst be the night when first I saw his bedd,
Curst be the time , the place, for now I see
It was my mony that he woed not me
And curst be all my thoughts that though so vaine
ffond love, to love what cannot love againe. exit

Actus jus Scena 2da
Ente Musophilus in the habit of a waterman
and ffido wth him

Mu: — Tis very straunge that amongst all misfortunes I should
be so fortunat as to meet wth, you;
ffi: — I am very glad to meet ⟨w⟩th you so soone after your returne
ffi: j [Fol. 2a]

ffi: But me thinks this habit doth not become you,
M: And why my ffreind doth not, guise beseem me

31 *A⟨n⟩d*] tear in paper 32 *manet*] ink spot to left of *m* 34 *releive*] *r* altered, from ?*h*; ascender visible 38 *Nuptiall*] *N* altered from *n*; tear between *a* and *l* 39 *vncha⟨r⟩itable*] tear through word from *v* to *i* 40 *His*] *H* torn *life*] *l* heavily inked; tear between *f* and *e* *coffers*] *c* written over something else 41 *⟨Curst⟩*] tear between this and preceding line, which leads up to line 39 *d⟨i⟩d*] tear over *i*, but dot and part of minim still visible 42 *bespedd*] *b* altered from ?*v*; blot below *s* 44 *time , . . . place,*] commas added in paler ink 47 *love,*] comma added in paler ink 49 *Musophilus*] waterspots above this word *waterman*] *n* different ink, very faint 51 *straunge*] *g* altered from *d* *I*] altered from *⟨.⟩e*, possibly *we* 52 *fortunat*] partially obscured by dirt and fold in paper *you;*] *y* and *u* added in different ink 53 *⟨w⟩th*] hole over first letter, probably *w* *you*] small hole on descender of *y* *so*] small hole on descender of *s* *returne*] page torn between *n* and *e*, but *e* still visible 54 *ffi: j*] previous line begun and abandoned but not cancelled 56 *, guise*] *g* touches comma

In this I am both wrechlesse, and vnkowne to vulgar
eye.
ffi: Na pardon me I did not censur but desire to know
Why being borne and bredd mongst schollers lawes
You have the vniversity and freinds forsaken,
And to the sea and waves, your selfe betaken.
Mu: Most faythfull freind, be assured that I am the very
same Musophilus, changing my habit only not my fayth
nor name, time and place, cannot alter my affections
this life [wch] to me doth seeme most pleasant,
The Ocean serves to moralise my sport
The waves wth sympathy did seeme to swell
to teach vs human men humanity.
I'th tides I see the wreched state of man
Is never standing ne'r at setled rate
But still doth rise and fall, all as the maine,
That Ebbs to flow, and flowes to ebb againe,
ffi: And as vnconstant as wavering fortune,
Mu: yet ffortune I acuse the not,
Let others plaine I never felt the changing
Bad wert thou at the first and so th'art still,
Befor I knew what's good, I knew the ill,
ffi: Sir you speake as though you wer melancholly
Relate your greife to me, do not conceale it,
I'le bear a pt although I can not salve it
Mu: My ffather hath tied the knott of all my sorrowes
But heaven knowes when he will vnty the same.
ffi Time and perswasion will mollifie, his stony nature,
By my entreaty cease to be sorrowfull,

57 *wrechlesse,*] comma added *vnkowne*] *v* heavily inked 60 *Why*] *W* heavily inked, ? altered from *N* *mongst*] retraced 61 *You*] *Y* inked twice *forsaken,*] comma added 62 *betaken.*] full stop added 63 *that*] ^{1}*t* written over something else 64 *fayth*] *f* faint 66 *to*] interlined above deletion with caret *seeme*] *s* altered from *y* *pleasant,*] *t* heavily inked, and line curving to right visible beneath; comma added 67 *serves*] final *s* blotted *to*] *t* heavily inked 68 *The*] *T* crossed but not fully cancelled; *he* heavily inked *sympathy*] ^{1}*y dotted* 69 *humanity.*] *i* heavily inked; full stop added 71 *setled*] *t* altered from *l* *rate*] *t* altered from *l* 72 *fall,*] comma added *maine,*] comma added 73 *againe,*] comma added 74 *ffi:*] water spots over *i* and to right of speech heading; ink blot to right of speech heading *fortune,*] comma added 75 *not,*] comma added 76 *others*] *s* smudged 77 *still,*] comma added 78 *what's*] apostrophe added later *ill,*] comma added 80 *me,*] comma added *it,*] comma added 81 *although*] *u* altered from *g* 82 *sorrowes*] ^{1}*o* blotted 84 *mollifie,*] comma added *nature,*] comma added 85 *entreaty*] *ea* altered?, letters blurred; ^{2}*t* lacks bar *sorrowfull,*] comma added

I'l cease to care, and so my thoughts I'l ease,
And lesser cares, shall greater cares appease,
ffi: boy Com we will drinck one cupp of wine, to welcome you hom
An drowne care in the midst of it,
Mus: All griping knawing cares wch do torment me
I'l⟨e⟩ wipe and wash away wth this Nepenthe. drinks.
Let vs goe and consider what course of life to take

Actus. j^{us} Scena 3^{tia}
Cremulus. Cremula

Cre¯lus The report goes that my sonne Musophilus is returne⟨d
even as he went a poore scholler
Crē la They say he is a good scholler and hath made
good vse of his time,
Cre̅u̅lus So let him and Ile mak good vse of my mony
I thank my starrs I was never cutt out
for a scholler, O t'is vnthriftiest thing th⟨is
learning.
Cremula This Owle cannot indure the brightnesse ⟨of
sunne, the greatest enemie to knowledg ⟨...
ignorance exit
Cremulus Tis too late now, I was going to take possess⟨...
your land wch you have iustly forfeted
Ti. Doe not exact the rigour of the law, heere[s] is your [Fol. 2b]
principle and your vse is doubled ,heer pray tell it over,
Cremulus. Well for this once I care not if I take it, come
let vs go in and tell it over in my privat house
– ffor heer we [both] doe suspect and feare
Each eye intentive, and attentive eare
This is my life my ioy, heer you may veiw

86 *I'l ... ease*] speech heading for Musophilus omitted *care,*] comma added *ease,*] comma added 87 *appease,*] comma added below original full stop 88 *boy*] interlined with caret and runs into *C* of *Com* *wine,*] comma added below original full stop 89 *care*] *c* blotted *it,*] comma added below original full stop 91 *I'l⟨e⟩*] faded *drinks*] *d* altered from *D* 95 *returne⟨d*] bottom right corner of page torn, part of *d* visible 97 *good*] *oo* left open at top *scholler*] long *s* altered from *sh* 98 *good*] *g* imperfectly formed; *oo* left open at top 101 *scholler*] long *s* altered from short *s*; *c* altered from *h* *th⟨is*] bottom right corner of page torn 103 *Cremula*] *a* altered from *u* *Owle*] ?*w* written over something else *brightnesse ⟨of*] bottom right corner of page torn 104 *knowledg ⟨...*] bottom right corner of page torn 106 *now,*] comma added *to*] *t* written over another letter; ascender visible *possess⟨...*] bottom right corner of page torn; entrance for Timothy may also be lost with tear 108 *Ti. Doe*] top of page cropped along top of these words 109 *,heer*] comma written close to *heer* 112 *doe*] interlined above deletion with caret *suspect*] *ct* retraced *and feare*] added in paler ink 113 *intentive,*] comma added

The sacred graft of the Hesperian tree.,
These goulden apples much the eye delighting
Would tempt the hands the longing tast inviting.
Oh now I could wish my selfe invisible or all
people blind.. exeunt

Actus j^{us} Scena 4^{a}
Musophilus.

This is my ffathers house and heer I'l try
What true affection he doth harbour in him [brest]
T'was henc that first I received my vnhappy being
That armes me wth [some] some confidence
And howsoer my genius doth præsage a bad event
Yet, I will persist and try the vtmost of his paternity
I now could greive although my greife I show not
I feare the more because my feare I know not
But resolution chids the daring teare
And courage make poor feare afrayd to feare
He is my ffather and I his sonne why then should I doubt
I know the worst t'is but my labour lost. tick tock — enter Vnice
Vni: Who's ther what would you have
Mu: If my ffather be within tell him Musophilus
his sonne craves entrance
Well heer I'l stay wth a resolution, to heare, and
wth patience to vndergoe his strictest sensure,
And though my duty cannot move his affection,
yet I will leave it behind me as a monument
of my obedience,
Vnice S^{r} He sayth you ar welcome, Mu: O ioyfull newes.
Vnice That is [if y] if you have brought any mony, from the
Indies other wise he says his house is not for beggers,
Mu: How's this no penny no Pater Noster, like

115 *The*] *T* altered from ?*t* *tree.,*] comma added 117 *tempt*] ?*pt* written over something else; brown dot visible above *p*, but may be stain or blemish in paper 119 *blind..*] second full stop added 121 *Musophilus*] ²*s* blotted, and inkspots on line and below 122 *and*] large ink blot above 123 *What*] *W* altered from *w* *him*] *m* altered from *s* 125 *That*] *t* altered from ?*l* *some*] interlined above deletion; *s* written over long *s* of *[some]* 133 *labour*] *b* heavily inked 135 *tell*] *t* imperfectly formed; *e* altered from *l* 137 *resolution*] another letter visible under or just before *r*; ?*l* or *t* 140 *monument*] ¹*n* blotted, and *o* slightly blotted 142 *Mu:*] interlined with caret; line separating speech heading crosses comma and caret 144 *Indies*] *i* damaged by tear 145 *How's*] page torn between *o* and *w* *penny*] *p* altered from ?*P* *Pater*] *P* altered from ?*p* *Noster*] *N* heavily inked

Diogenes his vultur alwayes expecting a pray
I know the worst I did his nature sift
When freinds ar gone I for my selfe will shift.
Now I'le set my invention on the tantur hooks
My witts I see are my best freinds and I had
rather be out wth all my freinds then out of
⟨.⟩y witts. But see heer cometh on whom by
...⟩⟨u⟩re and desert I may iustly call a freind
...⟩ my bended knee, I crave your blessing
...⟩ ⟨b⟩etter pt of me rise vp and stand
...⟩ds not crave who may my blisse command
...⟩ld weepe and spend that shortned breath that
...⟩rds me in cursing fate wch makes my
...⟩ short, I am so short winded as I
...⟩ call him roge and rascall both in a
...⟩ most sencelesse most inexorable

| enter Cremula.

| She makes as if she wept

[Mu: You wrong your self and me these] [FOL. 3a]

Mu: You wrong your selfe and me these idle teares
Quench not my greif but add new kindled feares
The very conceit of your affection, that only hath kept
life and soule together otherwise like discontented
partners they had long sinc bine disunited.
I felt your kind embraces wch you neither saw nor[.]
felt, I saw and felt mor mirth and ioy, then if
I had had possession of the Arabian mines or had
bine stiled Monarch of the Easterne world.

Cre: He stopps his eares as vnwilling to hear my soft perswasion
In your behalfe I oft did promise good.
But he my vowes and all [my] ⟨my⟩ hopes withstoode

Mu: The most ravishing musick, that ever Apollo could
modulate could not move attention in Midas, theer
is no musick seemes so sweet to him as the tincling

146 *Diogenes*] *i* damaged by tear 149 *set*] ink spots above line 153 *...⟩⟨u⟩re*] minim visible to left of *r*, probably *u* *iustly*] *t* altered from *l* *freind*] *d* retraced 155 *⟨b⟩etter*] ascender of *b* visible at beginning of word *pt*] *p* altered from *s* 156 *command*] *mm* five minims 160 *makes*] *k* altered 161 *wept*] descender of another letter, ?*p*, visible below *w* 162 *[Mu: ... these]*] blurred rather than fully crossed out 163 *these*] *s* heavily inked, lower loop unusually large 164 *Quench*] ink spot below line; *n* partially obscured 166 *discontented*] ^{2}*t* heavily inked 167 *disunited*] ^{1}*d* altered from *s* 168 *embraces*] ^{1}*e* altered from *s* 174 *⟨my⟩*] possibly *our*; interlined above deletion with caret and runs into ascender of *h* of *hopes*; blotted and with inkspot above interlineation 175 *The*] ascender of *T* has second bar halfway down *musick,*] comma added

of mony that is his cælestiall, and true Pythagoricall
harmonie.,

Cre: Me thinks I now could rayle on all the kind
Oh who can sound the depth of vsurers mind.
Oh that I were -divorced from him, I love
not fetters though composd of gold, but he had
best be very cautulous where he lays his mony.

Mu: Yor words I confesse are seasond wth affection, but
I pray take no care for me. exit

Cre: Adeiw if now I see the last farwell
Within thy brest all ioy and quiet dwell exit

Actus 2^{dus} Scena j^{a}.
Cremulus Crusophilus Genius

Sonne your very looke speakes you welcom, and I pray
be assured of it, you have already possession of your
ffathers hart, and hereafter shall have free possession
of what is more his goods and chattells [wh]

Cru: What must I say. Genius, to answer him and winn
his love

Geni: The only way to procure his love is to present the
bagg of mony that you received for the vse of that mony he
gave you to set vp your trade first, never feare, but
It will be restored duble and treble present it to him
and say, most kind and carefull ffather, Your dutifull sonne
hath brought you a small remembrance,

Cru: Well I'l go to him, Most dutifull ffather, your
kind and carefull sonne, hath brought you a
small remembrance,, Genius -Genius- calls him

Ge: What say you to Genius You can doe nothing without
Genius except it be telling of mony, and that you
will never imploy me in, your owne Genius will
serve you to doe that well enough,

180 *Cre:*] speech heading positioned between lines 180 and 181 181 *who*] *w* altered from *h* 183 *not*] *n* altered, from ?*h* 184 *best*] ascender of *b* extends below line 185 *Mu:*] colon has dash rather than dot as lower element *seasond*] *a* altered; ascender visible *affection*] ^{2}*f* faint 194 *his*] altered from *my* 197 *the*] *t* altered from *a* 198 ^{2}*of*] interlined with caret; *f* obscured by *t* of *that* 200 *will*] *ll* altered 201 *carefull*] stroke before *c* deleted with diagonal strokes; ink spot above *Your*] *Y* altered from *y* 202 *remembrance,*] comma added 203 *your*] *u* interlined 205 *remembrance,,*] second comma added 206 *What*] *W* retraced; *t* heavily inked *say*] *s* altered from ?short *s* 207 *it*] *t* retraced

Crus: thay say my brother Musophilus is returnd and lives by his [witts] w,w w w w, I cannot hit ⟨.⟩t.

Ge: By his witts. [Fol. 3b]

Cru: O ay ay some such thing. well, it's no great matter I thank God I was never so basely brought vp as to live by my witts, I can pay for that I have and that's honesty

Cre: Pray sonne let me see you oftner, you brought your welcome along wth you, O how this bagg fatts my desire, how it feedes my appetite, but the greatest care remaines how to convey it lest it be not seene I durst not trust in my house, my wife searches every corner of it, and heer is a place freest from suspicion, ly still my care, as for my neighbour Timothy his frivolous vowes and prayers shall availe him nothing, I forgave the forfetur of his band once and if I doe so againe, I desire that mony may fall to five ith hundred, let him find out my sonne Musophilus he will be a fitt companion for him now his mony is gone, in the meane time I'l go setle my selfe in his house and I hope his land will yeeld me a faire crop of corne next yeare exit

| exit Cru: Genius manet Cre |

| lays his mony over the beame |

Actus 2^{dus} Scena 2da
Musophilus . Simplicius
at severall dores

this is my way to the court

Mu: but see Yonder comes Simplicius Ile speake to him, now Learned Simplicius who art countenauncd wth Ladies smiles and great mens plaudits, the hope of preferment hath fully possest me, and I desire you would further my appetit wth a blast of your favour.

Sim: Preferment thou talkst as confidently of preferment as

210 *thay*] *a* imperfectly formed, possibly for *e* *Musophilus*] *sophilus* interlined with caret in different ink; *p* blotted *is*] *i* obscured by caret *returnd*] *ret* written over something else 212 *By*] written in thick, heavy, larger letters 221 *house*] *h* altered? 229 *gone*] *n* has extended preliminary loop 230 ^{1}*his*] mark to left of ascender of *h* *a faire*] ink spot on line beneath 233 *Musophilus*] second, heavier version of *Musophilus* written over first 235 *this … court*]: interlined 236 *but see*] added in left margin and crowded against *Yonder* 239 *would*] *w* retraced 240 *favour*] small mark before the word 241 *Preferment*] *f* faint *preferment*] *t* retraced

if thou hadst freinds and mony good store, (for desert let
that alone for future ages) is this the high way to
preferment to come vnder the forme of a poore man
what art thou

Mu: A scholler.

Sim: And can you speake Latine

Mu: No, but I have letters testimoniall that I am a scholler

Sim. This is a monster a scholler wthout Latine, the very crows
pisse latine (my grandfather sayd) at the Vniversity.

Mu: I can speak a litle, as much as crow did to Cæsar, but
I pray what office have you in the court.

Sim – I am the court mirth whom rude and saucy people
call foole

Mu: They distinguish now adayes ther be naturall [ffooles] and
artificiall [ones], ther be tollerable fooles and intollerable ones

Sim: Ther be fooles in ordinary and extraordinary ones
to speak truth ther be so many we can scarce
live on by a nother,

Mu: Now I'l vse a litle Latine, there be fooles cū privilegio
and sine privilegio

Sim I thought you had not lost all your latine, the best
course is to set vp a brokers shop of Latine, and
the next Aldermans speach that's made you may peradventur
light of a customer.

Sim: if not I'l make the Deane of Dunstable and that gratis [Fol. 4a]
too wthout any simonie , or sirra dost thou heare thou
shalt be a Iud,ge canst thou sleep well vpon a bench,

Mu: As soundly as Endimion, but wth a vigilant nose

Sim: Or thou shalt be a Burges canst thou tell the clocke

Mu: Very perfectly at my fingers ends

Sim. Thou shalt be a Bishop hast thou any great thums
canst thou say grace and yet if thou beest not a good politian

242 *freinds*] *f* heavily inked; *s* added in paler ink 243 *is*] retraced *to*] ink spot on ascender of *t* 246 *scholler*] *s* altered from ?*c* or ?short *s* 250 *at*] *t* retraced 251 *litle*] *t* retraced 253 *court*] ink spots before and above word *whom*] ink spot above *w* 254 *call*] ink blot under *a* 255 *distinguish*] ^{1}*s* and ^{2}*s* blotted 260 *vse*] ink spot to left of *v*; *s* imperfectly formed *there*] *re* added in paler ink *be*] interlined with caret in paler ink 261 *and*] *a* altered from long *s* *sine*] *e* loosely formed *privilegio*] *p* imperfectly formed; ^{3}*i* altered from *e* 262 *not*] *n* imperfectly formed *lost*] *s* imperfectly formed 263 *brokers*] ^{1}*r* imperfectly formed; ^{2}*r* heavily inked *shop*] *o* retraced *Latine*] *L* altered from *l* 264 *speach*] *p* altered from ?*c* 265 *light*] *l* altered from *y* 267 *simonie,*] *s* retraced 268 *Iud,ge*] *ge* possibly added after comma 269 *As*] *A* retraced? 270 *Burges*] *s* imperfectly formed 271 *Very*] *V* altered from *O* 273 *grace*] interlined with caret; *g* in paler ink, imperfectly formed *polititian*] *l* inserted

thou ar not fitt for the court.,
Mu: As good as ever Machivel,
Sim: But far well I had almost forgot my self I must
go to a Phisician, my wife is sick,-
Mu: If that be all then rest your selfe contented, I am
Asculapius his cheif scholler, you may go as farr as
Rome, the Antipodes Hercules his pillar [and yet] for Phisick
and yet not come ny me.
Sim: It's no matter farr you well I'l trust ner a scholler, of
you all to feele my wifes pulse
Mu: Mistrust not my loyalty, if she loves no flesh on ffridays
let, [l.t] her take three ounces of the Popes holy shadow
Sim: No she is rather [too much] a Puritan then a Papist.
Mu: I have a holy thisle and some other soveraigne medicinss
and vpon Saturday I will helpe her greife
Sim: Bewarr what you doe she is very precise and will not take any
Phisick on that day least it should work, on the Sunday.
But I shall not neede to trouble you, if she doth not mend
I'l send for you exit
Mu: Adeiu to your Nodiship, tis good to have foole to my freind somtimes
ffor though that wanton boyes do mock and flout them
The best and wisest have ther fooles about them. exit

Actus 2^{dus} Scena 3^{tia}
Timothy solus wth a rope

I can hardly indure wth patience my present adversity
if I doe but looke back vpon my former [adversity] prosperity
I that was so lately free from the cluches of a, cruell
extortioner, so willingly to fall into such a daungerous
relapse as this, thus to be stiled the scorne of men
and laughing stock of fortune, when as he like a

276 *far*] *a* blotted or altered 277 *my*] *m* blotted or altered 280 *for Phisick*] interlined above deletion; *P* partially obscured by deletion 281 *and yet*] added in margin in darker ink 282 *farr*] ^{2}*r* altered, from ?*e* 283 *you*] *y* written over beginning of another letter *my*] *m* altered from *th* 285 *let,*] in left margin in paler ink *the*] *t* retraced *shadow*] *d* blotted 289 *Sim:*] *S* altered from *M* *Bewarr*] ^{2}*r* altered from *e* *is very*] interlined with caret in paler ink, obscures *s* of *precise* 290 *day*] interlined in paler ink *work,*] comma added 291 *But*] *t* heavily inked *to*] interlined with caret *trouble*] *tr* blotted 292 *exit*] *x* blotted 293 *Adeiu*] *i* added in paler ink ^{2}*to*] *t* retraced *my*] *m* altered from *th* 298 *patience*] *t* and *c* very similar, but *t* has slightly longer ascender 299 *my*] *y* imperfectly formed *prosperity*] *adversity* deleted and *prosperity* added, both in paler ink 300 *a*] retraced 301 *extortioner,*] comma added *daungerous*] *r* blotted, ? altered from *t* 302 *stiled*] *s* imperfectly formed

cunning faulcner did display his lure, but hidd his
fist to cach me as his pray, na I was constrained
to pawne to him all that ever I was worth for this poore
peece of execution; this short spunne thredd of mans
mortality, now I thanke the Cremulus in this thou hast
given me a generall acquittance, In this I will
performe the office of a Iudge, a Iury, and
[shall] last, of there transcendent officer,, heer is that/ [turne over]
was inventd for the purpose I think

[Fol. 4b]

Ti: And since I am brought to this extremity I'l end
end all in this extreame line of mans humanity,
And then I am sure I shall never want
more, I ne'r can hope my losses to repaire

And he that cannot hope must needes dispaire

offers to hang him self and tying the knott of the rope finds a bagg of mony and leaves the rope ther

me thinks I am loth to goe so soone though.
How's this a bagg of mony, t'was well that I playd
loth to depart my musick had bin quit spoyld else,
especially my singing, her's mor then thangmans
wages sure, but sinc I am so well payd for my work
aforehand too, I care not if I leave it vndon, but stay, let
me looke peradventur I ioy without a cause, may be, it is
but a lightning before death, It seemes to be gould,
nay, it is gould, and I doe not think but it is ould
Cremulus that hidd it heer, but I wo[un]nder he will be,
so long from it, O fortune now I acknowledge the
to be more propitious vnto me then ever thou wert
therfore I will consecrate 4 butts of Sack to the
at Devill in St Dunstones, me thinks earths globe

304 *lure,*] comma added 305 *was*] *s* altered from *st* 306 *to him*] interlined with caret 307 *execution*] *x* and *t* heavily inked or altered *short*] *s* blotted or altered 308 *mortality*] ^{1}*t* heavily inked or altered *I*] added in paler ink *thanke*] *k* altered 309 *this*] *is* altered from *e* 311 *[shall]*] altered before deletion *there*] *th* altered *officer*] *r* altered from *s* *that*] ^{1}*t* altered from *a* 312 *inventd*] *d* obscured by blot at end of word 313 *Ti:*] bar of *T* heavily inked *end*] added in paler ink, then blurred 317 *him*] interlined with caret 318 *tying*] *y* altered 320 *thinks*] *k* altered from *ck* 322 *depart*] *t* altered? 323 *especially*] *ll* blotted *thangmans*] downstroke of *t* heavily inked 325 *not*] interlined with caret in paler ink 328 *think*] *k* altered from *g* 329 *wo[un]nder*] ^{2}*n* interlined *will*] *w* imperfectly formed 330 *from*] *f* imperfectly formed *acknowledge*] *g* altered from *e* 332 *4*] blotted or altered 333 *Devill*] top of *D* retraced *Dunstones*] top of *D* retraced

is too too angust to circle in my boundlesse [prayse] ioyes.
But I am constrained to epitomise my mirth.
I would say more of this but that I feare me
All waching Cremulus would overheare me. exit

Actus 2^{dus} Scæna 3^{tia}

Musophilus disguised like a souldier

I think my ffather can hardly know me in this habit
Mu: I'le try his charity as a straunger, heer he comes
wth his spectacles on his nose ⟨as⟩ I take it reading
som bill or bond, his sight failes him vsurie in a
man is lik the spleane the greater it waxeth the
lesser the limbs are.

enter Cremulus

Cre: The title is good alas poore Timothy would I knew
wher to have another of the price.
Mu: Pray sir let the silver thredds of your golden
compassion bind vp the decayed wants of a poore
souldier
Cre: Away away a souldier, that's almost as badd as a scholler
Mu: If it please you to show your liberality I shall thinke
my selfe holy devoted and mancipated to your extensive
munificence
Cre: Away away you cant.
Mu: Wth but blowing my nose I disipated a hole armie
of Persians.
Cre: Show me that trick and I'l give the mony enough
Mu: How much will you give me
Cre: A farthing
Mu: I will not refuse your liberality although you are too
prodigall,
Now have you not blowne them all away do you see
any body

takes him by the nose and pulls of his spectacles

Cre: O my spectacles the very same spectacles my ffather [Fol. 5a]
leaft me, O vnhappy man that I [⟨a⟩] am yet nothing
greives me but I must buy another paire, ah cheating

338 3^{tia}] The scribe has made an error in the numbering of the scenes here and in the following scenes. This should be scene 4 342 *⟨as⟩*] altered from *no?* *it*] interlined with caret in paler ink 345 *are*] *e* altered from *t* 351 *souldier,*] comma added in paler ink *badd*] *b* imperfectly formed; ^{2}d imperfectly formed, added in paler ink 353 pen strokes in left margin 356 *I*] ink spot to right of word 358 *the*] *t* retraced 362 *prodigall,*] *d* blotted; ink spot beside word 366 *I*] blot beside letter 367 *paire,*] *i* altered?; comma added

souldier, my spectacles , my eyes.

Mu: Why what's the matter you ar well enough if you can see ha ha he

Cre: O that I could find him whether is he gone I'l.–––– –

Mu: Ha ha he find him without eyes. ha ha he. exit *leave the specacles on the stage*

Cre: Vnice come quicly and see who is heer that hath got my spectacles from me

Vni: Heer is no body, but your selfe sir.

Cre: Then the knave is vanishd away

Vn: O master heer lyes your spectacles,

Cre: Birlady thats good luck , I am very glad he got not this paper away, well I'l stay no longer for fear he should come againe. exeunt

Actus 2dus Scæna 4a

Cremulus

This sam scurvy souldier had almost made me to

lookes and finds nothing but the rop

Cremulus forget my greatest care, O now my treasure, I can never think my selfe safe but when min eyes are fixt on the,

Oh me I am vndon I think the souldier hath bine heer also, he hath taken away my mony and hath not so much as left me a bill of his hand for it, only this small remembraunce, of all my mony heer is but poore [t]thirteenpence ob

enter Cremula an ffido talking together

Cremula I hope he is well.

ffi: And he protesteth he can never be vnmindfull of your vnfained affection

Cremulus ffor brevities sake I care not if omitt my confession:

offers to hang and is prevented by ffid and Cre

ffi: But stay what prodigious sight is this, oh fie Cremulus lay violent hands vpon your selfe and be accessary to your owne death

368 *souldier,*] comma added in paler ink *spectacles* ,] comma added in paler ink 369 *if*] blot after word 371 –'––– –] ellipsis evidently indicates Cremulus' inarticulate threats 375 *Heer*] *H* altered *body,*] comma added in paler ink *but*] *b* altered from long *s* 376 *knave*] *k* altered from ?*v* 377 *spectacles,*] comma added in paler ink 378 *luck* ,] comma added in paler ink 379 *away,*] comma added in paler ink *well*] *w* blotted or altered 381 *4a*] really scene 5 383 *This*] *T* altered from *C* 386 *but*] *bu* altered from *wh* *when*] *w* altered from *h* 391 *remembraunce*] *u* blotted 396 *omitt*] *o* retraced, slightly larger than usual 397 *is*] *i* is dotted *a* 398 *ffid*] *ff* altered 399 *violent*] *v* altered?

Cremulus Torment me not I beseech you

Cremula. Why this was beyound expectation to be so vncivill, as to offer to hang your selfe, without the consent of your wife and children you never knew them so vnkind as to deny you so small a curtesie,

Cremulus I pray be silent add not sorrow to sorrow, heape not greife vpon greife , O I have lost all my mony, I am vndon for ever vndon,

ffi: I am sure if you had not bine vndon you had bine vndone befor this time, come take comfort greife will not pay your losse. exeunt

Actus 2^{dus} Scena 5ta

Timothy solus

Ha ha he me thinks I could laugh my selfe in to my first principles, Oh my hart tripudiats and leaps for Ioy, I overheard in what perplexity the old croane was when he saw his mony was gone [Fol. 5b] he was much beholden to me who bequeath him so sufficient a legacie so long befor my death. Oh now my ioy is compleat me thinks it doth exuperatt his wonted bounds, and can hardly containe it selfe within the præcincts of a narrow bosome

Oh now I'l drinck I'l sing I'l roare I'l play,
ffor heaven hath sworne to make this holyday

My boone companions and cavaleiroes, I'l be wth you presently, exit.

Actus 3^{tius} Scæna ja

Musophilus ffido

Mu: Now ffido what's the best newes how goes the state of this miserable world

ffi: Y^{our} mothers prayers do attend you in all your enterprises, but your ffather was in suspension whether

401 *I*] altered from ?*b* 403 ¹*your*] *y* altered *selfe,*] comma added in paler ink ²*your*] *u* has only one minim 404 *you*] *y* altered? 407 *not*] *t* added in paler ink 408 *mony*] *m* has four minims 410 *this*] *t* retraced 411 *pay*] *p* poorly formed 412 5ta] really scene 6 414 *thinks*] *k* blotted 417 *saw*] *w* blotted 421 *containe*] *c* altered from ?*r* 423 *play,*] comma added in paler ink 425 *cavaleiroes,*] comma added in paler ink *I'l*] inkspot below word 431 *Y^{our}*] *Y* written over two lines, slightly to left of main body of text, and interferes with initial letters of two following lines; *our* written slightly above the line 432 *enterprises,*] comma added in paler ink

he should have hangd himselfe or no
Mu: What for the losse of a paire of spectacles
ffi: No t'was for a greater losse then that, but omitting
these things what course of life dost thou intend, to
runne
Mu: That blind ffortune leads me in, I have no mony, yet as free
from troubles and crosses as an Emperour,
ffi: The Proverb tell vs that he most is blest,
wch in this fragile life is crossed lest,
Mu: If that be true then fortune I defy
I am most happy for never a crosse have I,
ffi: What willtyou turne Player. Mu: No:[n],
ffi: will you be a gentle man vsher to my Lady Mince
One who is well knowne in Court, and very kind
and curteous to hir servaunts,
Mu: No that's as bad as a player, for ther a man should
overact him selfe I feare, No⟨,⟩ I had rather turne
preacher for I could bump a pulpit stoutly and
snifle through the nose devoutly, and then I am
sure I should have more followers then the greatest
potentat, in all the land, though I should chance to be
layd vp for a litle false doctrine yet ther contribution
would follow me to the deepest dungeon but there is
so many of these already, Therfore if all faile I'le to the
Court, there is the only place of preferment, besides a
freind in the court is as good as mony in my purse
ffi: But you must have mony in your purse before
you can have your freind in the court.
Mu: Simplicius is my trusty freind already, but I doe not doubt
but I shall procure more, every lord or knight, that
passeth by me I'l observe him and praise (and so as I'le be sure
he shall heare) on for his comly lock and heare, another for

434 *the*] *t* retraced 436 *to*] mark on line below *t* in paler ink 437 *runne*] ^{1}*n* blotted or altered 438 *That*] *t* retraced *leads*] *l* altered from *r* *free*] *f* heavily inked 440 *blest,*] comma added in paler ink 441 *lest,*] *l* altered from ?*b*; comma added in paler ink 443 *I,*] comma added in paler ink 444 *willtyou*] *t* rubbed out? *Player*] *P* altered from *p* *No:[n],*] colon written over deleted *n*; comma added in paler ink 448 *player,*] comma added in paler ink 449 *No*] *N* altered 453 *potentat,*] comma added in paler ink *though*] *t* altered from ?*l* 455 *is*] followed by flourish like start of long *s* 457 *the*] *t* altered *of*] interlined with caret in paler ink 458 *freind*] *d* blotted ^{2}*as*] inkspot below 460 *freind*] *fr* blotted *the*] *t* blotted *court*] *c* altered from *r*; *r* imperfectly formed 461 *Mu:*] *u* imperfectly formed *doubt*] *o* retraced? 464 *lock*] *k* blotted

his hansom legg, [⟨..⟩⟨esse⟩] on for his witt another for musick
one man because he is faire and another because he's black
One man for his bashfulnesse another for his boldnesse [FOL. 6a]
And so by litle and litle scrue my selfe into ther
good opinions.

ffi: I like this well this is the common practice - of this
age:

Actus 3^{tius} Scena 2da

Hillarius. Bond his clark. Musophilus.

Hi: Bond Bond have you writt the Indentures over
heare will be my Clients by and by wth full mouth.

Bond It's no matter so they come wth fulll hands too, but I
doubt I shall scarce have time to please them all
without helpe

Hi Is ther never a Clark heer abouts that wants emploiment

Bond: No: but ther is a poore scholler that frequenteth this
place much, who wth his own intelligence and some
litle teaching will prove an expert Clark,

Hi: But are you sure he can speake false latine otherwise
he is not for my purpose, one peece of true latine,
may be the overthrow of a hole cause

Bond: After once or twice walking to West minster he will soone
learne that for all false Latine, is confiscated to the
vse of Westminster hall,

Hi: Besides he may procure great store of Clients [to]
[Westminster] by his eloquence

Bond: But there [⟨.⟩] is another impediment makes me
thinke he will never be good Lawyer, he is so poore.

Hi: So much the better his want will make him speake the
more powerfully

Bo: But he liveth in great necessity, and you know very well

467 *bashfulnesse*] *a* blotted; *s* retraced 470 ^{2}*this*] *is* retraced 474 *over*] *r* written over *?* 475 *Clients*] *s* smudged 476 *It's*] apostrophe blotted or deleted *fulll*] ^{2}*l* and ^{3}*l* run together 478 *without*] *w* altered 479 *ther*] interlined in paler ink *abouts*] *bo* retraced 485 *cause*] *u* interlined with caret 486 *twice*] *w* blotted or altered *West*] *W* imperfectly formed 487 *Latine,*] comma added in paler ink 489 *Besides*] large caret in left margin, blotted and faint 491 *[⟨.⟩] is*] letter smeared, possibly cancelled beginning of another word 492 *Lawyer*] *r* imperfectly formed 495 *Bo:*] *B* altered from *d* *know*] interlined with caret in paler ink

necessity hath no [law], law, but see how opportunely
he comes *enter Musophilus*

Hill: He hath a good ingenuous look I'le speake to, save
you S^{r} how ffar walk you this way

Mu: But to the court,

Hi: Doe you hear he hath freinds at the court also,
and I pray what proffession are you of,

Mu: S^{r} I thinck I am scholler, or at least I goe
muses awhile for one

Hi: Schollers ar lawlesse but will you leave that, and
turne servaunt to a Lawyer, your service shall
neither be burdensome nor vnprofitable,

Bond: Doe. better be a clark then a petticurate
I know not what belongs to law yet I'le try.
Your knowledge is theoreticall mine practicall

Hi Come tim calls away to your businesse exit

Mu: But I pray tell me my M$^{[rs]}$aste^{rs} name [Fol. 6b]

Bond His name is Hillarius

Mu: Every tearme wth him is Hillarie term, and what is
this bagg for, is ther any mony in it,

Bon: No It is but a bag⟨g⟩ of my office come let vs go try
what Iuice my Master Seller yelds, I must fuddle
this younge Puny to welcome him. I'l warrant him
I'l teach him Law termes enough, [⟨bu⟩t] and first
instead of fee tayle he shall have a fox taile

Mu: Com let vs goe in, I feele wealth and honour com
stealing vpon me I shall be a Iustice of peace
ere long I know

Actus 3^{tius} Scena 3^{tia}

Timothy. Carowse, Lais, Bebia,

Ti Com Monsieur Carowse be merry, what shall we spend the

499 *how*] *h* altered from *t* *walk*] *k* altered from ?*l* 502 *proffession*] *ff* altered from *ss* 504 *muses awhile*] possibly added later *for*] *f* altered 506 *Lawyer*] *r* altered from *s* *your*] ink spot above *y* 509 Lacks speech heading for Musophilus? 510 Lacks speech heading for Bond? 511 *Come*] *e* retraced 515 *for,*] comma added in paler ink 516 *It*] *I* altered from *i* *bag⟨g⟩*] *b* altered from *s*; ^{2}*g* obscured by blot 518 *Puny*] *P* imperfectly formed 521 *Mu:*] written slightly below line *vs*] *v* malformed *in,*] comma added in paler ink 522 *shall*] *s* retraced 525 *Bebia*] *B* heavily inked; *b* altered from *d* 526 *Monsieur*] *nsieur* interlined with caret *be*] *b* altered from ?*m*

best of our dayes in sadnesse, and wholy devote our selves to that infernall deity mellancholly, com speake what wine will you drinke,

Car: The wine, Sake pure Canarie or non, Sirra, Boy,

Boy Anon anon sir

Ti: Bring vs vpp but a Gallon of Canarie first to tast lest it should not be right

Boy You shall S^{r}.

Ti: But what's the reason you are not merry, mounsieur ther is no dæmon but mellancholly

Ca: Troth I doe thinke ther is not any true mirth without the fæminin gender, and then if you will, it shall be impiety or petty treason to be sadd, each frowne a stabb to the others hart,

Ti: Thou art a man of my diet. (Enter Boy) how now sirra ist good wine,

Boy It be not as good as ever you drunck then let me turne bruers horse and never draw any thing but beare

Ca: Hast thou ne'r a hansom wench to iest withall,

Boy. Truly S^{r} we have non in our owne stable, but ther be too or three at the next dore,

provide me a good dinner of such kinds of meat as will strengthen me both backward and forward and call vs when t'is ready, but first, do, ye

Ti: Hear try if thou canst procure ther companie.

give hī mony Com let vs drinck, let vs not loose our time,
Wth mirth we will outire this day, the night
Wth ⟨G⟩ales of Nectar I will put to flight
Heer they com already whispering some pritty witty lascivious talk or other,

enter Lais Bebia.

Bebia How shall we demeane our selves modestly, or

527 *dayes*] *y* altered *wholy*] *w* altered from *h* *selves*] dot over *v* 528 *that*] interlined with caret, both in paler ink 530 *Boy*] *B* altered from *b* 532 *Ti:*] *T* altered from *C* *but*] interlined with caret 534 *Boy*] *B* blotted or altered 536 *ther … mellancholly*] interlined with caret *ther*] *t* altered from ?*T* 537 *not*] interlined with caret 538 *impiety*] *iety* in paler ink 539] interlined *or*] *o* altered from *v* *each … stabb*] interlined with double caret; runs into *Enter Boy*, line 541 *frowne*] *n* blotted *stabb*] *bb* blotted 540] inserted in left margin with double caret 541 *Enter*] *E* altered from *e* *Boy*] *B* altered from *b* 547 *our*] *u* altered 549–50] interlined 549 [1]*of*] *f* obscured by *r* of *forward*, line 550 550 *both*] *h* obscured by top of ascender of *t* in *try*, line 551 *backward*] *w* obscured by top of *f* of *if*, line 551 *forward*] [2]*r* obscured by top of ascender of *t* of *canst*, line 551 *when*] *w* obscured by top of ascender of *t* of *ther*, line 551 554 *flight*] *f* retraced 555 *whispering*] *wh* altered *some*] *s* retraced 556 *Lais*] *L* altered from ?*t*

wantonly, I doe not like this too much modesty [commend]
commend the senat for ther gravity
Lais T'is very true indeed,
A wanton Nimph will more delighte them farr
These modest Nimphs they seem more chast then arr
Bebia Women ar all alik the difference this
The one seemes and is not th' other seemes and is
Lais Or if some ar not as we call it ill [FOL. 7a]
They want the power and meanes but not the will
Both Ladies y'ar welcom set downe, I p⟨ra⟩y
Ti: Weele make a Law that whosever ⟨af⟩te^{r} they have
drunk ther full cupp do not sweeten ther mouths
wth a kisse shall drink double,
Ca: Wth all my heart, (Drinks and forgets to kiss.)
Ti: What forget so soone mounsieur, t'is too late now, enter boy
Boy your dinner is ready, the cok sparrow, will be spoild
if you make not the more hast
Ti: Com let's go in our mirth shall be the same
And after dinner we mor lawes will frame. (exeunt

Actus 3^{tius} Scena 4ta

Musophilus. Pritty.

Mu: Ay this is a good and a lawfull fee simple I would [ki]
continue a Lawyer all my lifetim, if I might but
have such fees as this alowd me, I have profited
well [i⟨n the Law⟩] for so small a time, I have got
possession that's eleven points of the law, ther wants
only the point of honesty, Iungemus Issue. kisses her
Prit: O fy na indeed I'l cry a gentleman and vse
a woman thus, you rend my cloaths, look some body
will see vs,
Mu: O these women ar most willing when most vnwilling

558 *like*] *l* altered from *L* 561 *Nimph*] line crossing first stroke of *N* 564 *one*] inkspots before and above word 565 *it ill*] obscured by waterstain 566 *but*] obscured by waterstain 567 *p⟨ra⟩y*] obscured by waterstain 568 *⟨af⟩te^{r}*] *ft* obscured by waterstain, *r* interlined with caret 571 *forgets*] *t* retraced 572 *What*] *W* blotted, written over another *W* *soone*] *s* altered *boy*] *y* retraced 573 *your*] ink spots above *y* *will*] *w* altered 574 *hast*] ascender of *h* collides with descender of *p* of *sparrow*, line 573 577 *4ta*] altered from *3^{tia}* 578 *Musophilus*] ᴵ*u* written over long *s* 579 *would*] *w* blotted or altered *[ki]*] smudged beginning of stage direction in paler ink 580 *but*] *ut* blotted, and followed by blot in margin 582 *time*] *t* altered? 586 *thus*] *t* retraced 588 *when*] *h* altered from *e*

Like Phillis that woed her sweethart by flying | ente. Hill:
from him. | Bond.
Hill: How now what woeing my mayd these are your
schollers trickes, this is a plaine case, Pritty
I chardg you mayd com not neere him, | | exit Pritty
Bond: This is pritty I fayth, How now ffellow clarke
you mistake your law termes, for noverint
vniversi, amaverint vniversi, for habere ad rectum
habere ad lectum, I thought what an habeas corpus
you had gott ther,
Hil: Have you bridled [your] my horse yet, I must ride forth
Mu: I cannot tell how to go about it no more then
your horse.
Hi: Ha ha he a true scholler he can neither bridle
my horse nor mend my sursingle, he is not for my
service send him gone make him a passe, exit | Hill: Bond
| manet Mu:
Mu: Rather make him an asse,
How quicly the knave my master smelt me out
I wishd him hand fort, and Indeed I see no reason
but those that live by the Law should dy by the law
well I must be content I know my last refu⟨.⟩e,
Onc more to th' court Tis but one mispent hower
Els let me never see more goulden shower.

Actus 3^{tius} Scæna 5ta [Fol. 7b]
ffi: Mounsieur Silly
I wonder wher Musophilus, is my hart would
daunce to find him, I doe not desire to imitate
the temporising fly playing in the sunshine of
prosperity, neither can his poverty any way disanull
my affection; He hath my mind and hart and now I see
Ioy is no ioy bard from his company

589 *Like*] *L* altered from *l* 599 *Hil*] *H* poorly formed *my*] interlined above deletion *horse*] *s* retraced 606 *Rather*] *R* altered 607 *quicly*] *quic* altered?; *l* retraced 609 *those*] *s* altered, from ?*e* 610 *refu⟨.⟩e*] penultimate letter blotted, ?long *s* altered to *g* 612 *let*] *l* blotted; blot before word 615–17] waterstain affects first section of these lines 617 *playing*] *p* altered from *f* *sunshine*] ^{1}*s* retraced 618 *neither*] *n* altered from *h*

But stay heer cometh on who (vnlesse my eyes faile me)
is in a deepe passion, O t'is mounsieur Silly a famous
gentleman vsher, I'l observe him a while

Moun: O Cupid Cupid wher art thou Cupid,
Over head and eares in woefull love
Now Cupid for thy mothers dove
help help help:

ffi: What devout Mounsieur.

Moun: O you spoiled the goodest verse I was making
my moane to Cupid, love doe so scrach me
by the elbow, I am in love as they say but I
cannot tell who to be in love withall nor
wherfor, Over head and eares in woefull love
Now Cupid for thy mothers dove
help help —— ———

ffi: What would you think of that man who would
help you to the speech of Cupid, the king of hearts
Duke of desires Lord of love and controwler of
affections,

Moun: That's the very same Cupid I would speak withall
Over head ——

ffi: Peace leave your frivolous repetitions, if this will
ease your greife, I know one who by his skill can doe
greater matters then these, your starr shall conduct
wheer you shall meet him walking alone in this
place

Moun: I will give you for this the best horse in my stable

ffi: Gramercy Horse, heer you shall meet him within
this hower, and in him you shall see the mirrour
and wisdome in the largest volumne. exeunt.

Actus 3^{tius} Scena 6ta

Mu: I was going to the court and I met wth a companie
of indigent souldiers, every on of them dischargd his oth
and swore he could get no[.] pay, looke heer they com

624 [1]*Cupid*] ink spot below *C*; *p* blotted in all three instances of *Cupid* 625 *woefull*] *ll* smudged 626 *dove*] *h* begun but abandoned after *dove* 637 *to*] *t* retraced 645 *walking*] *w* and *g* imperfectly formed *this*] *t* retraced; *h* blotted 647 *Moun:*] *n* altered from *u* 649 *hower,*] *r* added over comma 650 *volumne*] *m* imperfectly formed 652 *Mu:*] falls between lines 652 and 653

againe, surely I have some putrified fflesh [that these]
[ffashion monging courtiers d] that these flies do so
hang vpon me, doe yee follow me by the sent
I wounder what you see in me that's worthy [yy] your entreaty

i S^{r}. we have found mor charity vnder such a habit as yours
then vnder the most magnificent robe of a ffashion monging courtier

2 We have bine wher we have done service for the [Fol. 8a]
common wealth, In sat Ilands,

Mu: I'm sure the salt of Sapience hath forsaken the
powdering tubs of your braines,

3 And not any of vs runn away, till we saw our betters
runne before vs,

4 Ther was on ffrenchman I cut of his [legges] head
and he runne away wth all his might and maine for feare
he should loose his life as well as his heade, he had not
runne above halfe a league but seriously considering wth
himselfe, that his head was off wth the very conceit died
Iudg you whether this was not cowardly done, before
I would have done soe – –

Omnes: This is true we ar all eye witnesse of it,

Mu: T'is very straūge that in so small a time being
resident amongst these should learne to be mor
expert in lying then the frenchmen that taught
them.

j But I pray sir will you be pleased to impart somthing
towards a Supper, we feele the very spirit of famine
moving within vs, and chiding our sluggish hands wch have
not procured necessarie releife,

Mu: Ye hungrie needy slaves I'l tell you of a Duke that
keepes open house

Omnes Wher wher

657 ^{1}*me*] ink spot below word *doe*] ascender of *d* added in heavier ink 658 *you*] *y* altered, from ?long *s* *that's*] ^{1}*t* altered, from ?*w*, or retraced *your*] interlined with caret *entreaty*] *aty* blotted 659 *i*] altered from *2* *S^{r}*] *S* blotted *we have*] ink spots below and between words *mor charity*] ink spot between words *charity*] *r* blotted; *t* blotted *vnder such*] ink spots above and between words 660] line cramped at bottom of page *vnder*] ink blots above word 664 *braines*] *n* poorly formed 665 *vs*] *s* possibly superscript 667 *4*] falls between lines 666 and 667 669 *loose*] *l* blotted 670 *above*] *v* altered 671 *died*] ^{2}*d* poorly formed 672 *whether*] ^{1}*h* imperfectly formed 677 *lying*] *l* retraced; *y* altered from *i* 680 *spirit*] *t* blotted 681 *sluggish*] *l* altered from *h*; ^{2}*s* resembles *c* *have*] *v* retraced 683 *needy*] *y* altered from *ie* 685 *Wher*] *h* altered from *e*

Mu: In Paules ther you may goe, and walke your belly
full. I am very glad I am so ridd of these ffrenchified exeunt souldier⟨s
rascalls, but I pitty them and ther necessity, well
now I'l go on my præ intended iourny, But heer comes
a most expected man in whose bosom lyes all my
treaseur ente ffido
ffi: My desire was to meet wth you musophilus, and
opportunity hath answered my expectation,
Mu: I am very gladd the occasion was so congruent to ⟨.⟩ny
ffi: There is one Mounsieur Silly a gentleman vsher
who is so struck wth the passions of love that verily
beleeveth ther is such a diety as Cupid if
therfor you can but ffollow him in this humour
t'will be rare,
Mu: Let me alone
But first I'l serve my self his doting after
My Bayt shall Cupid be my pray true laughter

Actus 3^{tius} Scena [7] 7^{a}
Timothy solus

Tis strange to see my fortunes so soone eclipsed
and obnubilated by the interposition of sordid
poverty, Lais will not com ny me now she knows

[Fol. 8b]

my mony is gone, she shunnes me, as a marriner dos a daungerous rock
where as befor she would runne
at the very mot[t]ion of my fingers, nay not vexes
me but the scurvy hackny will not trust me for on
dayes iourny, I am sur I have bine of the customers
she hath, Next vnto hell as hell I doe defy
This base degenerat slavish beggerie

686 *Paules*] *P* altered from *p* 687 *ffrenchified*] line for stage direction crosses *d* 688 *souldier⟨s*] *l* obscured by *d* 689 *rascalls*] ^{2}*a* altered from *l* 692 *treaseur*] *u* blotted, possibly written with an extra minim 694 *expectation*] *p* blotted 695 *⟨.⟩ny*] first letter may be *p*; line may be incomplete 698 *diety*] *i* altered from *e* 703 *Cupid*] *p* blotted or altered 704 *[7]*] written in paler ink, blotted 707 *obnubilated*] *t* altered from *v* *interposition*] ^{1}*t* altered from *r*; ink blots above and below word *sordid*] *s* altered 708 *poverty*] *v* altered? 709 *she ... rock*] interlined with caret ^{1}*a*] followed by rising stroke *daungerous*] *d* blotted or altered 710 *mot[t]ion*] *m* altered; *ion* interlined with caret *fingers*] *s* blotted or altered 714 *degenerat*] *n* poorly formed

my meanes wch swelld of late to mountaines, could
I have seene it did fore tell this great and horrid
tempest, O haplesse man whose greife doth ioy appear
Who ever lives in pleasure lives in feare,
I scarce, can hope, yet fortune I will try
And add some hope to hoplesse miserie.

Actus 4^{tus} Scæn i^{a}

Mu: Wher is this sam strange new bird, this goose wth
golden eggs, he must be cherisht wth som graine of
hope but not fedd too fatt.,

ffi: He will be heer presently his passion is a sufficient
character wherby you may easly know him therfore
I'l leave you, exit.

Mu: I long to see my purchase, I must be altogether
Cupidate and speak nothing, vnder the straine of
a Lover, heer he comes overuld by the passions of | enter
Omnipotent Cupid and captivated by his prædominancie | Mounsie'—
This sam is he whose mouth spits flaming fire
Whose heart like Ætna burnes wth love desire

Moun: Over head eares in woefull love
Now Cupid for thy mother dove
help help helpe.

Mu:—O most kind most curteous Cupid

Moun: What's that you say of Cupid you are not acquainted wth
him I pray sir are you,

Mu: I would not for more the I speak of loose that
interest I have in him

Moun: I will give all my estat for on halfe howers
acquaintanc wth

Mus: Let me feel your pulse, you ar deeply in love, but
can you tell the m^{rs} of your affections

715 *meanes*] *es* run together, imperfectly formed *mountaines*] *m* imperfectly formed 719 *fortune*] heavy stroke above *une* 721 *Scæn*] *æ* blotted 724 *fedd*] ^{1}*d* blotted or altered 727 *you,*] *yo* blotted; comma heavily inked 729 *nothing,*] comma concealed by *d* of *overuld* below 730 *overuld*] *u* altered? 731 *prædominancie*] line of stage direction crosses *e* 733 *Whose*] *W* heavily inked *burnes*] *s* blotted and unclear, ?*d* 737 *Mu:*] line connects low speech heading to line 737 *kind*] *k* blotted or altered *curteous*] *c* altered from *k* *Cupid*] *p* altered 738 *Moun:*] oblique stroke over *M*; *n* has three minims *What's*] *W* possibly altered from long *s*, ascender visible 743 *acquaintanc*] *t* and *c* very similar, *c* slightly shorter 745] blotted pen stroke in right margin *you*] *y* has long stroke before it

Moun: Troth ther are so many pritty soules I know
not wch to affect most.
Mu: Ther is a Phisicians Daughter on Mr Vrina
her very name will mak your mouth water
Moun: Mak water in my mouth, O Mrs Vrina, I but
Mu: will you cast forth a good word for me. … [...,] x
Mu: x I'l doe as many a court chapline
mak Divinity all Rhethorick for
your Lordship.
Mus: I tell the I'l make[s] her all to belove, the, she
shall never rest till shee meet the heere, but first
arme the wth some potent magick charmes
Moun: What be they my chaps would faine be chaumping
them
Mu: ffirst repeat these four words wth a loud voice [Fol. 9a]
Boreas exentrix diaphragma paralellagramon
Mou: Bores, centr granham, these words will scare her.
Mu: No I'l warrant you, next you must anagramatise
her name and sympathise your ouwne
Moun: Tie thies sies, I shall never hitt ont., I thinke it
were better, to mak her love me, to discourse lik a courtier
of the best horses that belong to the court, ffreck
spaniard, Pegg wth a Lanthorne, strawburies and cream
flebitte Otho, and such things as these will please hir
best,
Mu: This mans toung is a gentle man vsher it goe before
his witt.
Moun: Or if you will make me some fine witty verses, [⟨in⟩]
Mu: What of the Diamond that circleth her litle finger
Moun: Or of that sweet flower in her hande that's the
newest fashion for verses.

746 *soules*] ^{2}*s* faintly inked 747 *most*] *s* retraced 750 *M^{rs}*] *s* poorly formed 751 *me.*] full stop added ?, at time of deletion 752–4] written sideways (in paler ink) in the margin, marked with *x* between speech heading and speech; *x* at end of line 751 and *Mu:* interlined beneath *will*, line 751 mark location of insertion 753 *Rhethorick*] ^{1}*h* altered from *e* 755 ^{2}*the*] *t* altered from *s* 760 *ffirst*] *ff* run together *these*] *t* retraced 762 *granham*] *r* imperfectly formed 763 *No*] *N* imperfectly formed ^{2}*you*] *y* imperfectly formed 765 *shall*] *s* retraced 766 *mak*] *a* altered 769 *Otho*] *O* altered from *o* 772 *his*] *s* retraced *witt*] *tt* altered, from ?*st* 775 *Moun:*] *n* blotted *hande*] *an* altered from *ol* 776 *newest*] *n* blotted or altered

Mu: Of her as she walks in the snow.
Moun: Or of the letting fall of her muffe
Mu: I'l' make [an en⟨...⟩ium] a paper of verses of hir in generall [and briefly thus]
gives him a paper
Moun: Let me se the next time I meete her I'l sweare
I made them ex tempore[,] but you told me I
should see Cupid heere is, en all but on poor groate
Mu: Be content he shall appeare to you in this place, but you
must be content to be blinded least the beames of his bright
diety wth ther lustre should hurt dasle your weake eyes
Moun: But how should I see him then,
Mu: I tell you you must beleeve[.] t'is he, and if he
chance to strick you you must beare it patienly.
Moun: No by no meanes wthout he will promise to doe me
no harme,
Mu: You need not feare his stick is of the same wood his
arrowes ar made of,
Moun: If that be all I'l beare the burden, but what must I
say to her, ties thies sies.
Mu: I'l teach you that as you goe, afor I'l overtake you,
Moun: By all the court horses I sware I'l be merry
the towns our owne, I no triumphe. exit
Mu: Now I have his mony I'le ffit him for a Cupid
I'l coole my hot lover, I'l be his Cupid for this once
Ill for a man was that man ever plact, [who lik to]
Who like to Ianus is not double fact
That's an ill wind wch no-man good hath blown
Then hoist vp sayles this prise is sure min owne. exit

779 *I'l'*] two apostrophes; *l* altered, from ?long *s* *make*] *k* altered from *d* *[an en ⟨...⟩ ium]*] one of missing letters has ascender *a ... verses*] interlined ^{2}*of*] altered from *on* 781 *meete*] ^{2}*e* possibly added later *her*] *e* altered from *r* 782 *tempore*] *p* imperfectly formed ^{2}*I*] possibly written over something else 783 *groate*] *t* retraced 784 *this*] *i* altered from *e* 785 *least*] *l* altered from *c* 786 *wth ... lustre*] interlined with caret *weake*] final flourish, perhaps false start of *s* 787 *Moun:*] *n* imperfectly formed *I*] altered? 788 *must*] *u* blotted or altered *and*] *a* altered from *h* 794 *Moun*:] altered, from ?*Mu:* *If*] *f* altered from *l* *burden*] *n* imperfectly formed 798 *towns*] *tow* altered *I no triumphe*] unclear; *r* altered, ascender visible 799 *I'le*] *l* blotted or altered 802 *Ianus*] *n* altered 803 *ill*] *i* altered from *r* *blown*] *o* blotted, possibly *oo*

Actus 4.^{tus} Scena ^{2da} [Fol. 9b]

ffido solus

I long to know how Musophilus hath delt wth
Cupids darling, it will go hard but wth the sam limetwig
he'l cach a bigger bird then this, Noble Musophilus
follow him, yet me thinks I pitty the poore lover
I wonder how the eye of man, wch in other obiects
cannot erre, shoud even then be most deceived when
they iudge of those graces wch are but colours plact in
womens faces, to a true [⟨l⟩ye] eye the swan seemes a
swan, the crow, a crow, b[h]ut a doting lover thinks
his crow a swan, thus doth love turne light into darknesse [into]
[Night], and darkest night is lovers clearest day.
Each lover like Theseus runns headlong into a labirinth
reason is the thredd that lead vs out, but some, ther are
who [who] have lost that divine distinction twixt man
and beast, love like warr is only sweet to those who
never tasted it, ,yet still the poor courtier cries
wthout it all life and ioy is tædious, but let him
tell me more of his mind hereafter. exit

Actus 4^{tus} Scena 3^{tia}

Mounsieur Silly, blinded, Musophilus atird
lik Cupid

Moun: I am constrained to grope out my way, ha ha he,
I can but laugh at those kind of people, wch history
tells vs never could abid women, they wer non of the wisest sure.
If but a true loves ioyes they once did prove
they would love to live vnlesse live to love;
Me thinks I grow filthy heloquent already
Now for my Cupid most odoriferous Cupid
Now Cupid doe I turne to thee
To thee vpon my barehead knee

805 *4.^{tus}*] *4* written over another number; *tu* blotted 808 *the*] *h* imperfectly formed or altered 809 *Noble*] *Nob* altered, from ?*bl* 810 *poore*] *oo* imperfectly written 813 *those*] interlined with caret 814 *eye*] interlined with caret 815 *b[h]ut*] *b* altered from *th* 816 *light into*] interlined with caret 817 *and*] *a* altered *darkest*] *e* blotted 818 *Theseus*] *The* partially deleted *runns*] altered, from ?*w⟨.⟩l*; ascender visible; *run* blotted *a*] interlined *labirinth*] *t* possibly altered from *c* 819 *is*] interlined 821 *warr*] *rr* smudged *is*] interlined with caret 822 *courtier*] *t* retraced, altered from *c* 830 *could*] *c* heavily inked *abid*] *d* heavily inked *they . . . sure*] possibly added later *wisest*] *es* crowded 831 *prove*] *p* followed by stroke like start of an ascender 833 *grow*] *g* altered, from ?*k*

knee never barehead yet before,
befor I begged at thy dore
Cu: All haile mounsieur according to thy prayer
I heer am present great King of harts, what wilt thou wth me,
Cup: So it be lawfull I embrace it⟨,⟩ say on my darling.
Moun: Love.
Cu: A light matter, if that be all. but wth whome, M^{rs} [⟨D⟩]Vrina
I warrant you, poore soule she melts and consumes
away in love of you,
Moun: Yes I think so,
Cup: But first you must tast of that divine vertue wch is
in this stick, — thwick thwacke —
Moun: Enough Cupid, oh, I'l trouble you no longer [FOL. 10a]
Cu: I'lteach you your love lesson once over againe. thwick thwack.
Moun: O that I could but find my way and I care not exit
Cu: Well now I may be vncupidate, how this asse, hath
suffered himselfe to beaten for nothing, he had forgotte
his charmes, if he meet, I'l tell him a false Cupid appeard
because he had for gott his magicke, thus is a foole and
his mony soone pted, if he goes to Mrs Vrina, she will
not so much as give him audience, these thing are
able to breake a young setter vppe, I will be
present, and ther I'l muster vp my senses, and coniure
all my in tellectuall faculties into one centre, and
if fate crosse me not I'l have a share in Vrinaes
love . exit

Actus 4^{tus} Scena 4ta

Vrina Bobadilla, Edentula bend old woman

Vri: I wonder what mettall these lovers ar made of
surely not of an earthy nor of a watery
substan

839 *haile*] *h* imperfectly formed 842 *⟨,⟩ say*] ink spots before and after word, comma and *s* obscured *my*] ink spots above and below *m* 844 *matter*] *m* blotted; ink spots above word *[⟨D⟩]Vrina*] *D* altered from *d*, then deleted 849 *stick*] *s* removed by flaking of paper 850 *Moun:*] *n* has three minims *trouble*] *r* blotted 851 *Cu*] *C* altered from *M* 857 *Vrina … will*] written lower than rest of line 861 *tellectuall*] *3l* altered 862 *share*] *r* altered from *l* 865 *bend*] *b* blotted *woman*] *w* altered 866 *what*] *t* altered

Bob: No but ther metall is all fiery
Vri: But where is this metall cheifly seated
Bob: In the heart of a lover
Vri: Well heaven defend me from heart burning I pitty
those who nurse fier in ther bosome,
Bob: So would I wer ther not meanes to abate the feircenesse
of it,
Vr: Ther may be such a thing as sympathie twixt
man woman, but I cannot beleeve ther is such
a thing in the essence of nature as love.
Bob: But who is this that comes in his pontificalibus / enter Moun: wth a paper in his hand
let vs observe him a while,
Vri: He comes reeding of [s..h as] some merry thing
that pleases him well, he smiles to him selfe,
Moun: These verses will please hir if she can but
vnder stand english, I must sware, I made them,
And first her head it is witts cheifest treasur
Her face the obiect of all humane pleasure
Her front the seat of ma^tie her eyes
Lik blasing comets in the clearest skies
Her cheekes like blushing roses, and all know
Her lipps like shamfast strawburies doe show
W^ch vnto all do sweetly blushing tell
The rest more pleasant fruits do lower dwell:
Exellent good I could not a made better my selfe
full of eloquence if these will not move[.] hir
what will, but see wher they are, looke how they [Fol. 10b]
marke the postures of my body, I doe not thinke but
they smell the very wood I was beaten w^th, O most
Happy basting. would he had bet me thrice as much
looke what a loving sheepes eye she casts at me
That heart that languisht now in loves tormenting
Shall have both hearts desire and hearts contenting

874 *to*] *t* inked twice 875 *it*] *t* heavily inked or altered 876 *thing*] *i* altered from *e* *twixt*] ²*t* retraced or altered 877 *beleeve*] *v* blotted or altered 878 *in the*] interlined with caret; *e* runs into *ss* of *essence* 881 *let*] *t* altered *his*] *s* imperfectly formed 887 *face*] *f* faint *the*] *h* blotted; ink spots on word *obiect*] *ob* blotted, ink spots on word 888 *front*] *f* faint *the*] *t* altered *of*] *f* imperfectly written 895 *full*] *f* heavily inked, altered from *?ff* *eloquence*] ink spot below word 898 *wood*] *d* poorly formed 899 *Happy*] *H* altered, ?from *h* or *l* 902 ²*hearts*] *h* imperfectly formed

I'l draw nier, I can hardly containe my selfe, I
would faine be at it, well I'l speake ⟨..⟩to them first
Lady, and beuteous Vrina wch of you it is I know not
But sur I am she is worthiest because I lover,
Eden: How dare you most impudent lover thus contaminat
her sacred name wth your poluted mouth, name hir
againe and I'l pull out your throat and sacrifice
you too a kennell of hounds
Moun: Tis very straunge you should bite thus, and have never
⟨..⟩a⟨.⟩ a tooth in your head, then know I come wth authority
I have a warrant from Cupid himselfe
Eden: Sirra I'l Cupid you –
Vri: Peace Edentula what is your name and whence
are you
Moun: Ay you speake to the purpose, my name is Mounsieur
Silly and a courtier.
Vri: In good time mounsieur Silly and a Cou[.]rtier
Comfort ioy, hope for ever I deny the
I would not name the now but to defy the
Moun: This is a hard sentence,
[Edentu: You wth]
Vri: Edentula you wth the rest of your coadiutors
teach him his love lesson
Eden: Medæa menippa Sill Grulla, come quicly and helpe
to coole this hot lover
| ent 4 furies
| and nipp him
Moun: Can you love then.
Eden: Wee'l tell you whether she can or no. nips him
Moun: O thou wich thou bich thou spawne
of a Mermayde
Eden: Thou Hells breviary, thou Ætna thou chaos nay tugg
and tugg, my virginity is tough enough
Moun: T'was causlesse love that wrongd my inocence
W^{ch} when it prosperd pleasd my ravishd sense

904 *⟨..⟩to*] smudge may be a cancellation or a blot 905 *you*] ink spot on *y* 909 *out*] *t* altered *throat*] *th* possibly touched up in paler ink 917 *Mounsieur*] *M* altered from *m*, and smudged 919 *Cou[.]rtier*] *u* interlined above deletion with caret 921 ^{1}*the*] *t* retraced or altered 924 *wth*] *t* altered from *c* 926 *Grulla*] *u* imperfectly formed *quicly*] *l* altered, from ?*k* 927 *nipp*] ^{1}*p* imperfectly formed 931 *Mermayde*] *M* altered from *m*; *y* blotted 932 *Hells*] *H* written over *wic* 933 *tugg*] ^{1}*g* blotted or altered *virginity*] *v* blotted or altered 934 *wrongd*] *g* lacks tail *inocence*] *c* blotted or altered 935 *ravishd*] *shd* blotted

[FOL. 11a]

O vnfortunate man that I am so farr from loving
any more that I am out of love wth my selfe. exit | lets fall a paper

Boba: T'is very strange that iust as we wer talking of
love this outragious lover should come in.

Vri: And sure his mind wth strong affections tainted
lookt through his eyes as through a glasse that's painted

Eden: And thus to love ther beuties never movd him
But therfore beuties seemd because she lovd him.
I think in conscience I was as hansom as either of
both these when I was a young wench, oh I was
as plumpe as the grape, O happy who that got the
first branch of my maydenhead, that was as I remember
t'wixt foure and five yeares of age, but now I must
confesse I am growne an auncient bearer.

Vri: Heer be the courtiers verses I'l read these when I have
more leisure, but hark what musicks this, / one sings

ffond painters love is not a ladd
Wth bow and shafts and feathers cladd
Much sooner is he felt then seen
His substanc subtile slight and thinne
Oft leapes he from the glauncing eyes
Oft in the snowy mounts he lyes
Oft lurks he t'wixt the ruddy lipps
Thence while the heart his Nectar sipps
Oft in a voice creepes downe the eare
Oft hides his darts in goulden haire
Oft blushing cheeks do light his fires
Oft in a smooth soft skin retires
Often in smiles often in teares
This flaming heat in water beares
When nothing els kindles desire
Even vertues selfe shall blow the fire
[All] Love wth a thousand darts abounds

936 *lets*] *l* altered from *e* 937 *any*] dot over *y* 939 *should*] *s* altered from *c* 940 *tainted*] [2]*t* blotted or altered 941 [1]*through*] *r* blotted, altered from ?*o* [2]*through*] *h* altered 943 *therfore*] *t* retraced 945 [1]*was*] *w* blotted or altered 946 [1]*as*] *a* blotted or altered from *w* *who*] *ho* altered from *as* 947 *as*] *a* written over downstroke of *I* 948 *t'wixt*] apostrophe directly over *w* *yeares*] *y* blotted or altered 949 *auncient*] *t* retraced or altered 956 *glauncing*] *l* altered from *a* 957 *lyes*] dot over *y* 959 *Thence*] downstroke of *T* retraced, possibly altered from long *s* 961 *goulden*] *l* blotted or altered 962 *Oft*] *t* retraced

— Surest and deepest vertue wounds
Oft times him selfe becomes a dart
And love wth love doth love impart
y^{u} painefull pleasur, pleasing paine
y^{u} gainefull losse thou loosing gaine
Thou bitter sweet easing disease
How dost thou by displeasing please
How dost thou thus bewich the heart
To love in hate, to ioy in smart,
To think it selfe most bound when free
And freest in his slaverie.
Every creature is thy debter
Non but love som worse som better
Only in love they happy prove

Eden: Had I my teeth as I have had I would sing
as well the best, but now I cannot keep
time

Vri: Was it me he aimd at in this love song, me thinks, [FOL. 11b]
that love whose power I defyed wth a strong resolution,
doth distill it selfe through my sanguine vaines, may be,
it is but a fitt, wch doth no sooner appeare, but vanish lik
clouds at the morning sunne, I feare Musophilus had a
finger, int,
Howso'er the event of fortune I will try
Wth true patience expecting remedie exit

Actus 4^{tus} Scena 6ta

Cremulus Cremula Crusophilus
Genius

Cremulus Me thinks I wax dull my spectacles begin to faile
me, and the greatest comfort I can receive from them,
is, they [..i⟨r⟩e] make my mony seem bigger then it is,
Com hethe Crusophilus,

Cremula How this rascall feedes himselfe wth the very thought

976 *bewich*] *w* blotted or altered 982 *love*] *v* altered 983 *would*] *w* altered? 987 *whose*] *w* altered from *h* *defyed*] *y* altered from *ie*; ^{2}*e* interlined 988 *through*] *r* imperfectly formed *my*] *m* altered from *th* 989 ^{1}*but*] *t* heavily inked *fitt*] ^{1}*t* altered, from ?*rs* *vanish*] *v* blotted or altered, from ?*p* 992 *Howso'er*] apostrophe over *e* *try*] dot over *y* 993 *patience*] *c* smudged *expecting*] ^{1}*e* altered from *c* 998 *comfort*] *f* altered from *p*

aside of mony, I could find in my hart to curse him, but
that I fear he would live too long if I should he
complaines of his eye sight, as farr as I can see he sees
too well

to him. Now heaven blesse your eyesight, ther ar phisicians, no
doubt, who wth ther who wth ther precious vnguents, can
cleare your eyesight, and make it as perfect as at the
first

Cremulus. I had rather be blind all my life time then be at the
chardges of a Phisician ,vnlesse they will bestow ther
potions gratis, I'l not deale wth them, I cannot abide these
long apothecaries bills, oh how they desire to see gold
glister, they never cease working till they have purgd the
purse of all the excrementitious humours, Rather I
am resolvd to continue as I am, come neer my greatest
ioy, in the I acknowledg my selfe to be young againe, and
to avoid all futur strife, and least my other senses should
be deficient, heer take the totall summe of all thats
mine, it is full contained in this small space of writing.
all my meswages Cottages Tenements barnes brue houses
backhouses dovehouses hogsties all pasture, and arable land
what soever, together wth my spectacles, I had almost
forgot them, and the rest of my goods and cattels, as
for my sonne Musophilus vnthriftinesse is his portion.

Cremula O most pernicious vsurer, nothing but a meer peece of earth poluted wth blood
He acknowlegeth him to be his sonne but in affection
he vtterly denyes himselfe to be a ffather,

Genius . You must thanke your ffather for his kindnesse and studdie
to deserve it, [I must thank you for your kindnesse]

Cru: I must thank you for your kindnesse and studdie to
serve it

Cremula Me thinks I can not hat my sonne Crusophilus [Fol. 12a]
and yet I can hardly affect him, his brothers affection

1002 *curse*] *ur* malformed 1011 *will*] *w* altered, descender visible 1013 *long*] *g* lacks descender 1014 *glister*] *s* altered 1017 *and*] *d* altered, from ?*t* 1019 *take*] ink spot below *k* 1020 *in*] *i* resembles *o*, but is dotted *writing*] *t* altered 1025 *vnthriftinesse*] *r* blotted or altered 1026] interlined; line from *Cremula* indicates that her speech starts here *vsurer*] *v* blotted or altered *poluted wth blood*] crowded in right margin *poluted*] *t* blotted 1027 *acknowlegeth*] *c* altered from *k* *affection*] *ff* run together, but two descenders visible 1029 *You*] left arm of *Y* heavily inked; ink spot to left of *Y* *thanke*] *k* poorly formed *your*] *y* altered, from ?*h* 1030 *[I … kindnesse]*] scored through and smudged 1031 *I*] obscured by blot 1032 *serve*] lower part of long *s* cropped

shall alwayes have supremacie, Now I could curse my
selfe or nature for framing me a woman,
otherwise I might have bine revengd on this damnd
extortioner, but t'is no matter I can fitt him as
other women do ther blind husbands,

Cremulus. Well, now Crusophilus the hole burden lies on your
shoulders see you beare it strongly you must be the
staffe of my old age, and vnder propp my weaknesse
Though now I am weak and blind I hope at length
ffor to regaine in the my former strength.

Actus 5^{tu} Scena ja
Musophilus

Mu: Oh now I find my invention is growne too weake and
my vnderstanding debilitated, neither can any language
seeme pleasant in wch Vrina is not namd, each sillable of her nam
is mor precious then balsamum, this this name is able
to make the sunne retrograde, and planet=stricke the
celestiall dieties, O sweetest Vrina thou master=peec of
nature and arts cheifest architecture, thou caracter
of vertue thou centre in wch all humane affections
meete, thou felicity of the Gods above, Oh how I could
loose my selfe in the spaciousnesse of her worth,
She is her sexes glory, ther's non hate
Nor envy any, but all emulate,
Heer she comes, able to charme deafe hell wth a pleasing smile
He that would look vpon this nimphs sweet eye,
Would swear't a Temple vowd to purity. | enter Vrina

Vri: Heer I hope to be private Musophilus doth so haunt me
at home, alas I pitty him, yet could I entertaine
such a thought as love, I would offer my selfe at his
shrine. but see where he walkes pray heaven he heard me not,

Mu: Her beautie is so Angelicall, I may veiw it but dare not

1037 *revengd*] *d* altered from *e* 1039 *other*] *o* retraced 1042 *vnder*] ascender of *d* retraced 1044 *my*] *m* altered from *f* 1045 *5^{tu}*] *u* blotted *Scena*] *a* blotted 1046 *Musophilus*] *p* blotted; *u* has only one minim 1048 *debilitated*] ^{2}*t* altered *can*] *c* altered from *t* 1049 *w^{ch}*] *c* altered from *t* *nam*] *m* blotted or altered 1050 *balsamum*] *l* altered from long *s* ^{1}*this*] *t* altered 1051 *planet=stricke*] *p* altered, ascender visible 1056 *loose*] *oo* crowded together 1064 *home*] *e* formed as *c* or *t* 1065 *such*] *c* blotted 1066 *shrine*] *e* poorly formed 1067 *Her*] *H* ? altered from *ff*

tuch the same, sweetest Lady, I sweare by all the infernall
medioxiniall and supremest Gods were it not presumption
in me I would entitle my self your servaunt,
Vri: Scarce did his hayre betray his blooming yeares
But wth his budding youth his love appeares
But I should iniure my selfe if I should stay any longer
If these few words some litle sparkles move
How would the rest enflame my soule wth love
Mu: O short felicity, howsoe'r I must aknowledg my selfe
happier then the vulgar sort of people, for breathing
in that parcell of ayer wch is perfumd wth her sacred
breath, but had she stayd to have filld this roome wth her
awfull presence, my felicity, had bine beyound mans
aprehension.
Mu: Oh heavenly powers what have poore men, deservd [FOL. 12b]
that you should frame a woman, ay. and make hir
so lively? and so comly? why should you cloth them
wth such a pleasing shape, why should you place
Gould in ther hayre allurement in ther face
And that wch most doth vexe men you impart
ffire to ther burning eyes, ice to ther hart.
But I must not leave her thus, I'l follow hir
both, in body and mind, enter ffido
Now noble ffido your face speakes newes, be
breife in the relation of it.
ffi: Your ffather blinded wth ignorance and affection
hath setled his hole estate vpon your brother
Crusophilus.
Mu: I thought what my round capp and my sophisticall
gowne would come too, all you that be present,
courtiers or what degree so ever [⟨you..y⟩ of] studdie ,studdie,
hard, to be fooles, that you may wth the more facility
inherit your ffathers lands, ah vengeanc on him,

1068 *Lady*] dot over *y*; *y* heavily inked 1070 *your*] cramped; *o* altered from ?*a* 1072 *But*] *B* altered from *b* 1076 *short*] *t* retraced 1077 *breathing*] *in* four minims 1078 *ayer*] ink spots above word 1079 *breath*] *h* blotted or altered 1083 *you*] ink spot below *y* *ay*] dot visible above, to left of *y* 1086 *Gould*] ascender of *d* heavily inked 1089 *But*] *t* retraced *her*] altered from *you* 1092 *it*] *t* retraced 1093 *ffi:*] *ff* retraced 1094 *hath*] *t* retraced *setled*] *t* retraced 1096 *sophisticall*] *p* blotted or retraced 1098 *or*] *o* retraced or altered ⟨*you..y*⟩] obscured by blot ,*studdie,*] added in right margin in darker ink

would he had disclaimed me from being his, sonne or forgott to be so vnnaturall a ffather, but I must find a trick to salve all this. exeunt

Actus 5^{tus} Scena 2da
Vrina sola.

Me thinks the course of nature is quit inverted in me, I can hardly be perswaded, that I am the same Vrina I was before, surely either mind or place is altered, or both, my hart is taken from me and seated in Musophilus his brest, oh these schollers they have such pritty arguments to invade and tak captive the soules of poore silly women, nay he would prove me to be his by Logicke and Philosophie, all, the arts and sciences, are comprehended in the volubility of his touung, me thinks I see him courting me wth more then cælestiall complements I wish he would try me once mor, if I denyde him any more, let me pressd to death, and mad an example to all my sex, O how I could curse myselfe for being so womanish in flying from him whom I so much affected, in whose face the the volume of my ioy was fully enlarged wth what a pritty modesty he seemd to woe as it were a farr of, but wth pleasing circumstances

T'was love of him that first my soule bereft
That in me of me nothing there is left. ex⟨it⟩

Actu^{s} 5^{tus} Scena 3^{tia} [Fol. 13a]
Simplicius Musophilus

Sim: Now Musophilus tell me how thou hast livd ever since I saw you last

Mu: E'ne as many others dooe by my witts

Sim: By your witts then sure you are a greate husband

1103 *a*] poorly formed 1104 *2da*] *2* altered, from ?*1* 1106 *thinks*] *t* blotted or altered 1110 *Musophilus*] only one minim of ^{2}*u* clearly visible 1111 *have*] ink spots above word 1113 *Logicke*] *e* poorly formed *Philosophie*] *P* retraced or altered 1115 *of*] *o* retraced or altered *touung*] ^{2}*u* possibly *n* 1116 *then*] *e* very faint *complements*] *n* altered, ascender visible 1117 *denyde*] ink spots over *yd* 1118 *pressd*] *p* blotted; ascender of *d* blots *ss* 1121 *affected*] blot to left of word ^{2}*the*] *t* altered from *sh* *volume*] *v* altered, from ?*p* 1122 *wth*] smudged *what*] smudged *modesty*] *des* and *y* smudged 1125 *ex⟨it⟩*] *it* smudged 1126 *Actu^{s} 5^{tus}*] ^{s} 5 smudged 1127 *Simplicius*] *p* blotted; *c* blotted; *u* blotted 1128 *hast*] *ha* altered from *do* *livd*] *d* altered from *e* 1131 *By*] *B* retraced or altered *husband*] mark above *u*; *s* altered from short to long form

to make so litle go so farre, but dost thou hear Sirra
I have got my wife wth child by channce medly, and I
would entreate the to make me too or three eloquent speeches
to a Lord or too to be my gossips

Mu: But I have somthing [else] to begg of you,

Sim: I thought so by your very countenaunce, thou dost come
to begg my place dostthou, if thou dost thou art a foole

Mu: No but my businesse is thus,

Sim: Com let vs set downe I'l hear the in order, and Iudiciously
too though I say it,

Mu: In breife my ffather (whom wth patience I cannot name)
being struck [wth] in yeares, [⟨fea⟩ring] and his sight failing,
(would [all] the rest of his sences had had ther completnesse
in deficiency only [)] that so he might 'a' bine, but
a rude peece of clay without forme or life,) he fearing
dissention after his death,

Sim: How could he fear any thing after his death [s⟨et⟩led his
aside estat vpon him]

Mu: Setled his estate vpon him, if therfore you will
post to the court and begg him for a foole thou
shallt be richly rewarded, heer are the articles
against him. ,

Sim: Well but you must grease my wheele before you can / gives him
set it a going, exit / mony

Mu: Heaven prosper him, t'is pollicie in great men to mak
fooles ther speakers, [for though that children still do mock and flout thē
The best and wisest have ther fooles about them.]
Now my Vrina every minut seemes a tædious hower
wherein I have not seene thy beutie, this is the house / tick tock

Page Who's ther that knocks so audaciously,

Mu: Where^{s} you^{r} M^{rs},

Page: Wher you would be. [wh⟨..⟩]

Mu: Wher's that? in bedd?

1132 *to*] retraced 1134 *speeches*] ^{1}*s* inked twice, ?altered 1137 *countenaunce*] ^{1}*n* retraced; *t* altered from *d* 1138 *my*] *y* altered *dostthou*] *sttho* altered from *do you* 1140 *hear*] *a* altered from *e* 1141 *it*] two dots visible over *i* 1143 *[wth]*] altered to *in*, then deleted *[⟨fea⟩ring]*] *f* altered from *p* 1145 *deficiency*] ink spot on tail of *f* 1146 *clay*] ascender of *l* blotted by erasure of parenthesis above *or*] *o* retraced or altered 1148 *How*] *w* blotted or altered, from ?*i*; dot visible 1148–9 *[s⟨et⟩led ... him]*] heavily smudged 1152 *shallt*] ^{1}*l* possibly deleted *articles*] *c* retraced 1154 *but*] interlined over caret *wheele*] *l* retraced 1155 *set*] *t* blotted, or altered from *l* *it*] *t* blotted or altered 1157–8 *[for . . . them]*] lightly deleted 1160 *beutie*] *u* altered from *a* 1163 *[wh⟨...⟩]*] deletion smudged

Pag: A smelsmock ar you ther about, the naked truth
is my M^{rs} is not drest.
Mu: No matter boy, beautie when most vnclothd is clothed best
Prithe tell her heer is on would speake wth her
Page I will S^{r}. exit.
Mu: Now now if ever let my toung be tipt wth more
eloquence then ever Iove courted his fairest Alcmena wth / ente⟨.
Heer he comes the messenger, heavens forbid she should / Pa⟨..
wound me wth her non placet.
Pag: S^{r} my M^{rs} sayth she is not w^{thin} [Fol. 13b]
Mu: If she will come hether and say so I'l beleeve[⟨.⟩]her
Pag: Will you not beleeve me then.
Mu: No tell her Musophilus would speak wth her, | exit Page
but I feare that name is of no efficacie to move
attention, if he wer heer again⟨.⟩ I would invent a mor
pleasing name

enter Page Vrina, Musophilus and Vrina stand amasd –

Page. This is pritty sport he tould me he would speak wth
my M^{rs} but he'el not be so good as his word, look how
lik Images they, I'l lay my life they ar in
love, your lesser cares speak loud, but great ones
stand amasd.
Mu: Thus long have I rested in silent admiration, and
should I not vent it my hart would splitt in sunder
and loves fir were it any longer suprest, would vtterly
consume this corporeall ædifice, and mak my hart
combustible, my errant then is love? [⟨a p....pt..y err⟩]
Vri: A peremptory errant
Page: Well sedd Mrs I knew you could not be wonne wth
a wett finger,
Mu: Are you angry because you are beloved, couldst
thou indent wth beautie and desert how farr to

1166 ^{2}*is*] *s* altered from *n* 1167 *beautie*] *a* altered from *u*; *i* altered from *e* 1168 *Prithe*] *e* altered from *y* 1171 *Iove*] *v* faint *courted*] *t* not crossed *fairest*] *s* smudged 1175 *and*] ascender of *d* heavily retraced *say*] *s* heavily retraced *I'l*] *I* altered *beleeve[⟨.⟩]*] *r* or *v* deleted 1176 *Will*] ^{2}*l* blotted 1179 *again⟨.⟩*] final letter, ?*s*, obscured by blot *invent*] *i* blotted 1183] ink spot at beginning of line 1186 *your*] *y* altered from *l* 1187 *stand amasd*] cramped, possibly interlined 1188 *admiration*] ink blot at top of *t* 1189 *sunder*] *d* poorly formed 1192 *[⟨a p....pt..y err⟩]*] smudged 1196 *angry*] ink spot above *y* *couldst*] *l* heavily inked

extend, and set desire downe a limit wher to end I then might cease my suit.

Vri: I can love a litle,

Page . Is the wind ith that dore already

Mu: Could you cease from being Vrina, I then could cease from being your true affectionat musophilus

Vri: I can no longer dissemble nor shall your love returne empty but be associated wth my true affection

Mu: And I'l confirme it thus,/kisses her

Vri: And I thus \kisses him.

Mu: Thus hand in hand let vs too walke whom love hath so indissolubly ioned. exeunt.

Actus 5^{tus} Scena 4ta

ffido Cremula weeping

ffi: [ffido] have patience

Cremu: I'l pull out his eyes

ffi: You shall not need he's blind already,

Cre: I will studdie to be Rhetoricall in curses sinc I am so weake in revenge, when saw you Musophilus how doth he beare this vnwelcome newes

ffi: Wth a forct patience.

Crem: Patience, t'would make incivility ashamd, and put immodesty to the extent of a blush, to heare of his ffathers inhumanity

ffi: He might have given [him] Crusophilus the greatest pt of his [FOL. 14a] meanes as he was the eldest, but the lesse in respect of his vnworthinesse

Cre: Natur might be ashamd to place her priority on such vnworthinesse,

ffi: Blame not nature she observes an æquality, she gave the on a portion of land, the other a portion of witt.

1201 *Page*] *g* blotted or altered 1204 *can*] dot after word 1207 , *kisses*] comma possibly written over rule before word 1209 *in*] *i* altered from *v* 1210 *indissolubly*] *i* altered from another letter, ascender visible 1214 *Cremu:*] *C* written over something else; *m* altered from *C* 1219 *ffi*] *ff* retraced 1220 *ashamd*] *h* formed like long *s* 1223 *He*] *H* altered from *ff* *Crusophilus*] interlined above deletion *greatest*] ^{1}*t* retraced 1224 *eldest*] *l* altered 1226 *might*] *m* altered, ascender visible 1228 ^{2}*she*] *s* altered from *t*

Cre: Witt without mony is lik a bagg puddin without fatt
com let vs try if we can find Musophilus, in him
we will repeat the second lesson of our patience.

exeunt

Actus 5^{tus} Scena 5ta
Musophilus Simplicius

Mu: I wonder Simplicius stays so long it makes me
suspect the event, surely, he hath not wit enough to prove
disloyall, heer he comes, wth a cheerefull looke as if / enter
he bin successfull, now noble Simplicius have you / Sim:
spedd,

Sim: Doe you make a question of it, heer it is in black
and white, full power and authority to take possession
of all that you can call his, they laught at the reeding
of the articles, heer take, it I must leave you
for I have a suit of mine owne to ffollowe, but Sirra
dost heare I heard say thou canst coniure,

Mu: I have studdied the black art

Sim. The Divell you have, but can you tell me who
loves a wench best of all this companie, [B⟨an⟩ks]

Mu: Banks his horse could doe that, I'l tell the all
the spectators especialy those that doe not laugh
they that look as though butter would not melt
in ther mouths

Sim: Adieu madd wagg remember my speech. exit

Mu: Well now I am at the height of my wishes, heare
must my hopes be terminated, nor could I wish
kneele. a greater happinesse, heer comes a paire of the / enter
truest freinds that ever my bosome harboured, nor shall / Cremula
I be forgetfull of my duty and your curtesie / ffi:

1233 *lesson*] *l* altered from *s* 1234 *exeunt*] ink spots above and below ^{1}*e* 1238 *surely*] *u* altered, ascender visible *enough*] interlined with caret 1239 *disloyall*] *d* retraced or altered 1240 *he*] *e* altered from *a* *now*] *w* altered 1242 *question*] *q* altered, long descender visible *of*] *f* faint 1244 *reeding*] blot next to word in right margin; *n* imperfectly formed 1247 *coniure*] *u* has third minim 1248 *black*] *b* altered from *v* 1249 ^{1}*you*] *y* altered from *th* *but*] *b* altered 1250 *companie*] first minim of *n* deleted 1254 *ther*] *t* altered from *m*; *h* altered 1255 *Adieu*] two dots over *i* 1256 *Mu:*] *u* blotted or altered; dot over colon *now*] ?rust spot below and to right of *w* 1257 *be*] *b* altered, second ascender visible 1258 *kneele.*] dash connects stage direction with *truest*, line 1259 *paire*] *i* altered *the*] *th* altered from *m* 1258–60 *, heer . . . curtesie*] interlined, cramped

Cre: Now my wreched Musophilus [⟨m⟩]
Mu: Why wreched
Cre: Because your ffather made you so,
Mu: But I'l make my selfe fortunate, but where is
my ffather I have a great desire to see him
Cre: Why should you desire to see him who neither sees, nor
affects you | Mu: no matter I'l overcom good wth badd

Enter Cru: Ge: Cremulus ledd by his Mayd.

heer, he comes vnderpropt by a weake mayd Ile
observe him.
Cremulus When will the day appeare? shall I alwayes walke in
darknesse? making my life but on l⟨.⟩sting night

exit mayd

[Fol. 14b]

⟨.se⟩ ⟨...⟩nipotent Iove, is it thy iniustice, that makes me
b⟨...⟩ or is it my wickednesse wch hath deserved this
privation, couldst thou not at onc have deprived me as
well of life and being, as of my cheifest sence and facultie
Mu: He speaks sorrowfully I pitty him.

enter Vnice

Vni: Your Phisician sends you word that vnlesse you can
procure the water of an honest woman or of an
vnspotted virgin your disease is incurable,
ffid: A hard and investigable remedie,
⟨Cr⟩emula ⟨a⟩sid He's like to be blind still for all me.
⟨C⟩remulus. Entreat my wif no doubt but she is honest
.....⟩la: Alas I have gott the colique, you must pardon me
..⟩i: Can you mayd you have a good honest looke,
Vnice What a pritty senclesse question is ther, I am above
12 yeares old, and have livd in the citty all my life time
and could you expect it of me,

1261 *my*] *m* blotted or altered *wreched*] *w* blotted or altered *Musophilus*] ink blot below *us* 1262 *wreched*] large blot after word 1264 *my*] *m* altered 1265 *great*] ink spot below *r* 1266 *neither*] *n* blotted; *eit* retraced or altered 1267 *affects*] word poorly formed, ?altered; *ff* run together *Mu:*] interlined after stroke separating speech heading from previous speech *good*] *oo* imperfectly formed 1269 *heer*] *h* blotted *vnderpropt*] *v* imperfectly formed; *r* blotted *by*] written over *m* *Ile*] *Il* altered from *we* 1271 *When*] *W* retraced, preceded by vertical stroke *walke*] *k* blotted 1272 *making*] *m* altered, ascender visible *on*] ink spot below *n* *l⟨.⟩sting*] *a* obscured by blot 1273 *⟨...⟩nipotent*] ink washed off page at top left corner *iniustice,*] comma retraced 1275 *me*] interlined with caret 1276 *being*] tail of *g* written over comma? 1280 ^{1}*of*] ink spot after *f* ^{2}*of*] *o* altered, from ?*a* 1281 *vnspotted*] *vn* added in left margin, cramped 1282] interlined, cramped 1283 *⟨Cr⟩emula*] word damaged by water stain 1284 *⟨a⟩sid*] word damaged by water stain 1285 *⟨C⟩remulus*] word damaged by water stain 1286 *.....⟩la:*] edge of page torn off *colique*] *q* retraced 1287 *..⟩i:*] edge of page torn off 1289 *12*] written over *9* *old*] interlined over caret

Mu: I'l vndertake his cure, I know Vrina is as chast as
Diana. exit.
Cremulus Who was that wch spoke such comfortable language
ffido Musophilus
Cremulus It can not be I never deserved a thought of good from
him. and can ther be love in men beyound desert,
Cremu: I hope he spak in Iest,

ente Mu:
and Vri:
anoints Cre:
eyes

Mu: Com hether Vrina you shall see what vertue
there is in your water
Cremulus. Most welcome [⟨ni..t⟩] day, God morrow, let me know
and see the author of my felicity
Mu: Heer he stands, Cre: this act exceeds beleife, can it
bee that you can have so much charity, (I cannot call it duty)
to so vnkind a ffather, [T'⟨is . k..d..sse t⟩hat]
Mu: T'is a kindnesse sufficient the acknowledging of your
former vnkindnesse read this,
Cremulus What's this a grant of Crusophilus his land to you
Musophilus, begd for a foole
Mu: No, the foole beggd him for me
Cremulus To what our superiours yeeld I willing ly subscribe
Nay were not that sufficient I wodl revoake
my grant and bestow it on you.
Cruso: What must I say now Genius. (cryes
Gen: You may say they have made a foole on you
Mu: Be content I'l yeeld you an annuall pension
to buy you a fooles coate, now nought remaines
but that you would be pleasd to grace our
nuptialls wth your presence,
Cremula What marriag too sonne on fortune vpon the neck
of another,
Mu: This Vrina, this totall summe of chastity, is mine
[⟨t⟩he] in affection there wants only the ceremony

1291 *his*] *s* blotted or altered *Vrina*] *V* altered, from ?*D* [1]*as*] interlined 1292 *Diana*] *D* poorly formed, retraced or altered 1296 *and*] *d* blotted *can*] *c* obscured by blot 1298 *Vri*] *V* retraced or altered 1299 *what*] *t* blotted 1301 *[ni⟨..⟩t]*] deletion smudged, ?*night* 1303 *Cre:*] interlined with caret 1304 *you*] interlined with caret *duty)*] parenthesis retraced 1305 *[T'⟨is ... t⟩hat]*] smudged 1306 *sufficient*] *ff* crowded together 1307 *vnkindnesse*] *ss* crowded together 1312 *wodl*] looped ascender of malformed *d* may indicate deletion 1319 *nuptialls*] *nu* blotted or altered 1320 *fortune*] *n* blotted or altered

of marriage and your paternall consents
both: Be happie in your loves [Fol. 15a]
Cremulus. In this I'm gladd that I shall have a pt
I'l ioine your hands together the heavens your hart.
Mu: Thus to the Church we'el go when thou art there
Then t'is a Temple I durst bouldly swear
Wee'le all be merry, and our noblest guest
Will take ther welcome for ther greatest feast
I would say mor but that for this perhapp
The author sayth he feares an after clappe.

ffinis

[Fol. 15b blank except for name 'Thomas' and superscription]

1325 *Be*] *B* unusually large 1327 *together*] [1]*e* altered from *t* 1330 *guest*] *e* blotted or altered 1331 *Will*] *Wi* altered from *Sha* [2]*ther*] *t* altered from *g* 1332 *perhapp*] [3]*p* blotted